The
Virginia Presidents

A Travel and History Guide

Richard E. Dixon

Clifton Books

2014

Cover and Frontispiece: The Eight Virginia Presidents
(Courtesy of Bradley Stevens)

Copyright 2004 by Richard E. Dixon

Print   ISBN 978-0-578-14758-1

For

Richard III, Dorin, Alden, Ellen, Kelli, Samuel
Bradley, Paul, Victoria, and Adam

THE EIGHT VIRGINIA PRESIDENTS

(standing) John Tyler William Henry Harrison James Monroe

Woodrow Wilson Zachary Taylor

(seated) George Washington James Madison Thomas Jefferson

A painting of the eight Virginia presidents as they would have looked during their presidencies.

Used with permission of the artist, Bradley Stevens,

and of Bahman Batmanghelidj, who commissioned the painting by Bradley Stevens.

The painting has been donated by Mr. Batmanghelidj to Curry School of Education, University of Virginia.

TABLE OF CONTENTS

INTRODUCTION

This book is for the traveler interested in the lives of the eight men from Virginia who became President of the United States.

Four of the first five presidents were Virginians - George Washington, Thomas Jefferson, James Madison and James Monroe - covering thirty of the nation's first thirty-four years. Two - William Henry Harrison and Zachary Taylor - professional soldiers who would push aside the American Indian as America moved to the Pacific Ocean. One - John Tyler - would annex Texas and watch the nation break apart in Civil War. The last Virginia president - Woodrow Wilson - born on the eve of the Civil War, would try to infuse a concept of progressivism into a world order at the beginning of the twentieth century.

Two of the birth homes — Harrison and Wilson — and two of the birth sites — Washington and Monroe — may be visited. Two of the birth homes — Tyler and Taylor — still exist, but are in private hands and not open to the public. Seven of the presidents acquired homes during their life time, which have been preserved as memorials —Washington, Jefferson, Madison, Monroe, Harrison, Tyler, and Wilson — in which guides and exhibits tell the story of their lives and the nation that they served.

The lives of the eight Virginia presidents are told with special attention not only to their homes, but to the many other sites for each president that may be visited.

The purpose of this book is to provide the reader with the historical context of these presidential sites. The reader may go directly to a president or a site of interest. The Table of Contents lists all the sites associated with each president. This is the book I wish I had with me when I visited these many sites. I hope you will find it a helpful companion.

R. E. Dixon

Clifton, Virginia

June, 2014

British America

At the end of the 16th century, Spain was the dominant power in Europe, but England did not hesitate to challenge the Spanish in North America. Sir Walter Raleigh called the large, vaguely defined area of the east coast of the American Continent, Virginia, after Queen Elizabeth I, the virgin queen.

Raleigh sent over two colonies that settled Roanoke Island on the east coast of what became North Carolina. The first stayed one year (1585-86), and a second mysteriously disappeared without a trace, the fate of the inhabitants unknown, and today simply referred to as the "lost colony."

In 1606, James I of England gave charters to Virginia Company of London and Virginia Company of Plymouth to settle the entire east coast of the North American continent. A year later, 105 male adventurers brought by three small ships, the *Susan Constant,* the *Godspeed* and the *Discovery,* after an arduous four month voyage, landed on the coast of Virginia at **Cape Henry**. The ships moved up the river which they named for James I, and established **Jamestown**, the first permanent English settlement in America. By the end of the seventeenth century, English colonies occupied the entire seaboard from Georgia to upper New York.

To remove England as a rival, Phillip II of Spain launched the Great Armada in 1688, but the combination of hardy English seamanship under Sir Francis Drake and devastating weather doomed the Spanish invasion. This would mark the nadir of Spanish naval power, vault England into the preeminent power on the seas, and pave the way for expansion of the British empire in North America.

Clash of Empires

After the Treaty of Utrecht in 1713, the English controlled the eastern seaboard from Georgia to the Gulf of St. Lawrence, with the Appalachian Range as the western boundary. A large area between the Appalachians and the

1

A cross north of Virginia Beach marks the site where the James-town settlers first came ashore at Cape Henry on April 26, 1607. From this site can be seen the Chesapeake Bay where Admiral de Grasse blocked the English fleet from Yorktown.

Cape Henry and First Landing Monument

The place of the first landing in Virginia on May 6, 1607 by the Virginia colonists was on the south cape of the entrance from the Atlantic Ocean into Chesapeake Bay. It was named in honor of Henry, Prince of Wales, and the cape on the north side for his brother, Charles. A granite memorial cross marks the approximate site where the colonists landed. It is also opposite this site where the French fleet under Admiral de Grasse in the Battle of the Capes blocked the British fleet from the Bay and prevented it from relieving Cornwallis at Yorktown. A series of plaques, overlooking the Bay, illustrates the Battle of the Capes between the French and English fleets. A statue honors the contribution of de Grasse to the cause of American liberty.

Visitors: The site may be visited during the daylight hours throughout the year.

Directions: The monument marking the landing at Cape Henry is located in Virginia Beach on U.S. Route 60 at the north end of Atlantic Avenue. The site is located on Fort Story, a U. S. Army base, but access is permitted from U.S. Route 60.

Contact: Colonial National Historical Park, P. O. Box 210, Yorktown, Virginia 23690; (757) 898-2410; http://www.nps.gov/came/index.htm

Mississippi River remained in dispute. France retained the province of Quebec. It also kept Louisiane, a large slice of territory in the middle of America which became known as the *Louisiana Territory.*

British America was settled by families seeking a new beginning. As they multiplied they needed more land so be-

Historic Jamestowne - America's Birthplace

Jamestown survived its first disastrous years and remained Virginia's capital until 1699. At that time, the capital was moved to Williamsburg and Jamestown became unimportant to the commerce of Virginia and slowly faded back into the wilderness. When the Association for Preservation of Virginia Antiquities received 22.5 acres of Jamestown Island as a gift in 1893, only the 1639 church tower was left of the original settlement. The remaining 1500 acres of the island was acquired by Colonial National Historical Park in 1934.

In 1994, the APVA began an archeological search called Jamestown Rediscovery to locate the original fort which was thought to be under water but was found on the APVA property. The Jamestown Fort Excavation Site can be observed by visitors. At the Jamestown Visitor Center and Museum, there is a film, "Jamestown," a museum of artifacts and the ruins of Virginia's first industry, a glass factory built in 1608. The Glasshouse has been reconstructed with an operating glass works. Park rangers conduct tours, and there are cassette tape players for self guided walking tours or for auto tours. The site is jointly administered by the National Park Service and The Colonial Williamsburg Foundation on behalf of Preservation Virginia.

Visitors: Historic Jamestowne is open daily every day of the year (except Thanksgiving, December 25 and January 1). The front gate opens at 8:30 a.m. and closes at 4:30 p.m.

Directions: Jamestown is at the end of the Colonial Parkway which provides access to Williamsburg and Yorktown. From I-64 take exit 242A, then Route 199 west to the Colonial Parkway. It can also be reached by Route 5, then south on Route 31.

Contact: Colonial National Historical Park, 1367 Colonial Parkway, Jamestown, VA 23185; (757) 856-1200; http://www.nps.gov/jame/dex.htm and http://www.historicjamestowne.org/index.php

Jamestown Settlement

Jamestown remained the capital of Virginia until 1699, when the capital was moved inland to Williamsburg, at that time called the Middle Plantation. Jamestown Settlement is located near the original site. A movie, "Jamestown: The Beginning," will orient the visitor. The English Gallery describes the background for the colonization of North America by England and how the Virginia Company of London first sent three small ships to Virginia. The Powhatan Indian Gallery describes the development of Indian culture in the Virginia Tidewater from about 10,000 B.C. The Jamestown Gallery shows the growth of the colony from that first landing to the establishment of Jamestown as the capital of Virginia.

There is an Indian village and the re-creation of the 1607 triangular fort. A path leads to the dock at which are tied replicas of the three small ships, *Susan Constant, Godspeed and Discovery*. The visitor can go aboard and imagine crossing the Atlantic for 145 days with the prospect of landing on a barren shore. James Fort has been re-created to match the original fort. There are historical interpreters who speak about the activities of colonial life. Jamestown Settlement is operated by the Commonwealth of Virginia and is different from Historic Jamestown which is nearby.

Visitors: Jamestown Settlement is open daily all year except Christmas and New Year's Days from 9:00 a.m. to 5:00 p.m.

Directions: Jamestown is at the end of the Colonial Parkway which provides access to Williamsburg and Yorktown. From I-64 take exit 242A, then Route 199 west to the Colonial Parkway. It can also be reached by Route 5, then south on Route 31.

Contact: Jamestown Settlement, 2110 Jamestown Road, Williamsburg, VA 23185; (757) 253-4838 or toll free (888) 593-4682; www.historyisfun.org

gan the inexorable westward movement. They widened the Indian trails to roads, cut down the woods for farms, built towns and took over the rivers. The native peoples, long settled here, fought back. The French, desperate to keep the English settlements from reaching the Mississippi, allied with the Indians.

War flared again in 1739 and although an uneasy peace was reached, both England and France continued to covet the disputed area to the Mississippi River. France edged down from Quebec and England stretched its colonies westward to the Ohio Valley and they collided in 1754.

In that year, the French built Fort Le Boeuf, south of

Louisiana Territory

It was called Louisiane by the French and became known as the Louisiana Territory. Its eastern boundary stretched the length of the Mississippi River, from the Great Lakes in the north to New Orleans, then westward to the Rocky Mountains, over all the lands which drained to the Mississippi, Missouri and Arkansas Rivers. In 1672, a fur trader, Louis Joliet, with the missionary Jacques Marquette, rowed the Wisconsin River and then the Mississippi to where the Arkansas River joins. Ten years later Sieur de la Salle canoed the Mississippi from the Great Lakes to New Orleans and claimed all the lands which drained into it from east and west for Louis XIV. The French claim to New Orleans controlled access to the Mississippi and New Orleans.

Lake Erie. A young colonel from the Virginia militia, George Washington, rode out to warn the French this was English territory. On his return, he recommended to Lord Dinwiddie, Virginia's royal governor, that the juncture where the Allegheny and the Monongahela Rivers form the Ohio ("the forks of the Ohio") would be a good location for a fort.

He returned the next year with 300 militia men and found the French already at the site building Fort Dusquene (now Pittsburgh). Washington set up a defensive position appropriately called Fort Necessity. In a sharp engagement, the French proved too much for the Virginia militia and Washington was eventually forced to surrender.

Upset at the French intrusion, the English turned to their regular troops and they marched out under the command of Edward Braddock, the top British commander in North America. George Washington went along as an aide. His advice on how to fight the Indians was largely ignored by Braddock, who marched into a trap and died along with two-thirds of his force.

France Loses Canada

Over the next two years, England and France collected allies on the European continent and in 1756, the Seven Years War began, called in America the French and Indian War. It was for England a great opportunity to break the line from the St. Lawrence to the Mississippi and free the colonists to move west.

Under the command of Major General James Wolfe, the English forced the surrender of the French fort at Louisbourg in Nova Scotia after a seven week siege. Wolfe then sailed up the St. Lawrence to Quebec, found an unguarded path up the cliff to the Plains of Abraham and arrayed his battle lines.

The French, under the Marquis de Montcalm, marched out and deployed in the formal battle style. English discipline on the battlefield proved too much for the French and Montcalm was mortally wounded. The gallant Wolfe would also die on the field, soon after the French surrendered.

The loss of Quebec forced France to surrender its claims to North America. To save the Louisiana Territory the French secretly ceded it to Spain in 1762. England did not challenge this transfer, but in compensation, it forced Spain to give up Florida.

The Treaty of Paris in February, 1763 gave England control of all of Canada and America to the Mississippi River. It marked the zenith of British colonial power in North America.

The ten years that followed the conclusion of the French and Indian War witnessed a dramatic change in the attitude of British America toward rule by the "Mother Country." In the next decade, the colonists, once loyal subjects of the crown, became convinced that Parliament intended to take away or drastically curtail their rights as Englishmen.

The thirteen colonies in 1775

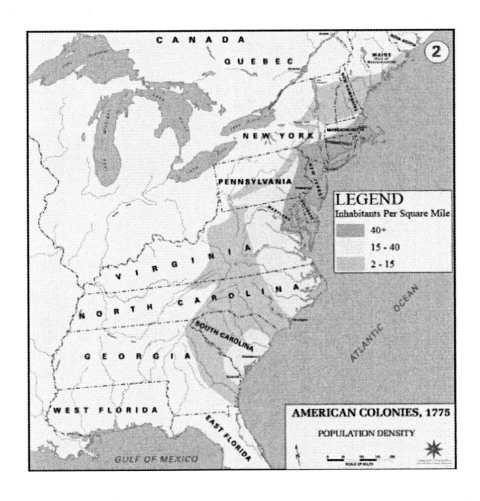

Rebellion

Great Britain looked to the colonies to pay its share for the French and Indian War, but the Americans felt no such obligation. They believed that the actions of Parliament made them second class citizens and even termed their fate as "slavery." British America had a long tradition of independence.

Although the colonies were started by "charters" from the king and were ruled by royal governors, they were settled by independent and free men, churches, and private investors.

Racial diversity was not an issue because slaves had no rights, and the colonists were united by language and religion.

Racial Diversity

During the colonial era, America's population began to diversify. On the eve of the Revolution, those of English origin comprised about half of the population. There were large concentrations of Dutch, Irish, Scots (about 20% from Scotland and Ireland), and German (about 10%), Welsh, as well as some Swiss, French and Jews. In the northern colonies, about 80% of the population were English although in Pennsylvania German and English were about evenly matched. In the south, in states such as Maryland, Virginia, North Carolina, South Carolina and Georgia, where the economy depended largely on slave labor, those of African descent averaged about 40 to 45% of the population. However, these non-English groups did not change the dominant influence of English culture, language and constitutional traditions. Religion played a central role in colonial society, where church membership ranged from 56% of the south to 80% of the north. Maryland had a large Catholic population, but most Americans were Protestant, with many different denominations and sects. Ideological values from a predominant Christian affiliation, English as a common language, and shared political traditions, provided unifying elements throughout the colonies.

In the decade after the French and Indian War, there was increased resistance to the authority of Parliament. The colonists first asserted their rights as British subjects. As the conflict with England escalated, the colonists came to believe that government was not legitimate unless it was created by consent of the governed.

Parliament Asserts Authority

Since the mid-seventeenth century England had controlled colonial America's foreign trade. In return, colonial ships enjoyed the protection of the British Navy and benefitted from a steady market at British ports. In 1762, England began to issue Writs of Assistance to inspect cargoes. This inflamed the merchants using the port at Boston and James Otis argued that these royal writs were search warrants and a violation of fundamental English law.

In July, 1764, in *The Rights of British Colonies Asserted and Proved,* Otis raises what will become an immutable principle of American political thought, that there can be "no taxation without representation."

Stamp Act. Parliament first passed Grenville's Sugar Act of 1764 to extend an existing trade law. That was followed quickly in 1765 with the Stamp Act to impose a tax on a variety of documents and activities, including playing cards, insurance policies, wills and other legal documents, advertisements, bills of lading and licenses. At the same time, the Mutiny Act (also called the Quartering Act) was passed requiring the colonists to provide rooms in their homes for the English soldiers.

In Williamsburg, Virginia, on May 29, 1765, Patrick Henry proposed to the House of Burgesses a series of Resolves which raised for the first time the argument that only the colonial legislatures and not Parliament could tax the residents of the colonies. At this time, Henry excited the state when he shifted his attack from Parliament to the King. To the cries of "treason" Henry retorted, "If this be treason, make the most of it."

The furor raised throughout the colonies and the economic impact on British merchants caused a repeal of the Stamp Act. Parliament then met the central issue of taxation of the colonies by passing the Declaratory Act, affirming the power of parliament to tax the colonies.

Townshend Acts. This was followed quickly by the Townshend Acts (named for the new prime minister) which levied taxes on glass, lead, tea, paint, paper, and many other imports to the colonies. The opposition was vehement, particularly in Boston, where a squad of British soldiers fired on an antagonistic crowd and killed five Americans. To retaliate, the colonists refused to accept English goods. At the urging of the new prime minister, Lord North, Parliament lifted the duties in 1770 on all goods except tea.

While on patrol to halt smuggled goods into the colonies, the British sloop *Gaspée* ran aground and was soon ransacked and set afire. The British issued orders for the perpetrators to be arrested and brought to England. This violated the ancient right to be tried by a jury of one's peers and caused an uproar in the colonies.

Committees of Correspondence. It was difficult for the colonies to coordinate their opposition because government officials were under the direction of royal governors. To establish contact outside regular government channels, Dabney Carr, brother-in-law of Thomas Jefferson, offered on March 12, 1773, a resolution to the House of Burgesses in Virginia, to create a committee to contact other colonies. These Committees of Correspondence, soon adopted by the colonies, set them on the road toward union.

Boston Tea Party. Then, in 1773, England tried to save the distressed British East India Tea Company from bankruptcy. Parliament removed the payment of duties so that East India could undercut both legitimate American merchants as well as the price of smuggled tea. The answer by the colonies became the Boston Tea party. A band of men, dressed as Mohawk Indians boarded the anchored *Dartmouth* and dumped its tea into Boston Harbor.

Parliament quickly retaliated. In March, 1774, parliament enacted the first of the "Coercive Acts," called by the colonists the "Intolerable Acts." It shut down the port of Boston until the East India Company was paid for the lost tea.

When word reached Virginia that Parliament had assumed authority to close Boston's port, the House of Burgesses adopted resolutions expressing sympathy to the people in Boston. Lord Dunmore, Virginia's Royal Governor, responded by dissolving the Burgesses, which adjourned to the *Raleigh Tavern* and called for a Virginia Convention.

Raleigh Tavern

Raleigh Tavern was established about 1717 and named for Sir Walter Raleigh. It grew to be the most popular location of social and political activities during the years preceding the Revolution. In 1774, when the news reached Williamsburg that England had closed Boston's port in retaliation for the Tea Party, the House of Burgesses immediately passed resolutions in support of Boston. Governor Dunmore retaliated by dissolving the Burgesses and the delegates walked down the street and convened a meeting in the Apollo Room of the Raleigh Tavern and called for Virginia's First Convention. The tavern burned in 1859 and a succession of stores were built on the site. In 1928 the buildings were removed and the original foundations were uncovered. Using drawings published in a book and insurance policy sketches, a replica of Raleigh Tavern, built on the original foundations, was opened in 1932. The property is owned and maintained by the Colonial Williamsburg Foundation.

Visitors: Colonial Williamsburg is open all year. Raleigh Tavern is open seven days a week but hours may vary depending on the season.

Directions: Williamsburg is at the halfway point of the Colonial Parkway which provides access to Jamestown and Yorktown. Williamsburg can be reached by Route 5, the John Tyler Memorial Highway or by I-64 from Richmond or Norfolk, take exit 238, Route 143, then right on 132 to the Visitors Center.

Contact: Colonial Williamsburg Foundation, P. O. Box 1776 Williamsburg, VA 23187-1776; www.colonialwilliamsburg.com; see also, www.williamsburg.com and www.history.org

In May, Parliament passed the Quebec Act. Although not in the series of Coercive Acts, the provisions alarmed the colonists, and was included by them in the measures by Parliament which America called the "Intolerable Acts." The purpose of the Quebec Act was to provide a permanent civil government for Canada, but it reserved the power of taxation to Parliament, a direct challenge to the position taken by the Americans.

Another provision that caused great resentment in Virginia was the claim that Canada's boundaries were to be extended to the Ohio River, over areas claimed by Virginia, Connecticut and Massachusetts. The next blow came in a new Quartering Act in June, 1774, which required citizens of all the colonies to provide sleeping accommodations and food in their homes for British soldiers.

First Continental Congress

George Mason rode from his home at *Gunston Hall* to Mount Vernon and gave George Washington what became known as the *Fairfax Resolves*. They were adopted by the Freeholders and Inhabitants of Fairfax County, at the Alexandria courthouse on July 18, 1774.

Washington submitted the *Fairfax Resolves* to the First Virginia Convention, meeting in the *Capitol at Williamsburg*. The Resolves expressed loyalty to the crown but called for a trade embargo against Britain until the siege of Boston was lifted. The Resolves also raised the need for the meeting of a "general Congress."

Natural Law. With English constitutional history as the foundation of his paper, a young Virginian, Thomas Jefferson, penned *A Summary View of the Rights of British America.* Jefferson went beyond the common argument that the colonists were entitled as Englishmen to be ruled only by their elected representatives. He berated the king for permitting the excesses of Parliament and asserted that the rights of the colonists were "derived from the laws of nature, not the gift of the king."

It's tone was a little too strong for the delegates as-

George Mason and Gunston Hall

The fourth George Mason was born at Dogue's Neck, below Alexandria on December 11, 1725. He was ten years old when his father died and he was taught how to run a plantation by his mother. In 1758, he built Gunston Hall, then a wheat and tobacco plantation of 5,500 acres overlooking the Potomac River just below Mount Vernon. He became an ally of George Washington in resisting the efforts of the British parliament to place internal taxes on the colonies. He wrote the Fairfax Resolves, which were presented by Washington to the Virginia Convention and they became Virginia's statement to the Continental Congress. A year later, he was the principal author of Virginia's Declaration of Rights, adopted by the General Assembly on June 12, 1776. This document was to influence the Declaration of Independence and became the model for the Bill of Rights. George Mason was a delegate to the Constitutional Convention in 1787, but his refusal to sign the Constitution because it did not have a bill of rights strained his long friendship with Washington. He was not a part of the new government and died in 1792, and his contributions faded from the public mind. The opening of Gunston Hall to the public in 1952, the dedication of George Mason University in Fairfax, Virginia in 1972, and the creation of the George Mason Memorial on the Mall in Washington, D.C. in 2002 has returned his name and his unique contributions to public prominence.

Visitors: Gunston Hall is open daily except Thanksgiving, Christmas and New Year's Day, from 9:30 a.m. to 5:00 p.m. Guided tours every half-hour; Group tours (703) 550-9220 Email: groups@gunstonhall.org

Directions: Gunston Hall is on the Potomac River below Mount Vernon. From Virginia Route 1 take Virginia Route 242. From Interstate 95 take exit 161 at Route 1, then north to Route 242.

Contact: Gunston Hall Plantation, 10709 Gunston Road, Lorton, Virginia 22079; (703) 550-9220; www.gunstonhall.org

sembled in Philadelphia in September, 1774, as the First Continental Congress.

Capitol at Williamsburg

Virginia's capital was moved from Jamestown to Williamsburg in 1699 and two years later the foundations of the new capitol building were started. It was completed in 1705. Fire gutted the interior in 1747, leaving only the walls standing. It was rebuilt, but when the Virginia capital was moved to Richmond in 1780, there was no use for the capitol building and it fell into a state of neglect. In 1832, fire again destroyed all but the walls. It remained abandoned until the first original building with its distinctive rounded ends was rebuilt by the Colonial Williamsburg Foundation. There is a plaque which reads:

Here Patrick Henry first kindled the flames of revolution by his resolutions and speech against the Stamp Act, May 29-30, 1765.

Here, March 12, 1773, Dabney Carr offered, and the House of Burgesses of Virginia unanimously adopted, the resolution to appoint a committee to correspond with similar committees in other countries - the first step taken towards the union of the States.

Here, March 15, 1776, the Convention of Virginia, through resolution drafted by Edmund Pendleton, offered by Thomas Nelson, Jr., advocated by Patrick Henry, unanimously called on Congress to declare the colonies free and independent states.

Here, June 12, 1776, was adopted by the convention the immortal work of George Mason - the Declaration of Rights - and on June 29, 1776, the first written constitution of a free and independent state ever framed.

Visitors: Colonial Williamsburg is open all year. The restored Capitol is open seven days a week but hours may vary.

Directions: Williamsburg is at the halfway point of the Colonial Parkway which provides access to Jamestown and Yorktown. Williamsburg can be reached by Route 5, the John Tyler Memorial Highway or by I-64 from Richmond or Norfolk, take exit 238, Route 143, then right on 132 to the Visitors Center.   Contact: Colonial Williamsburg Foundation, P. O. Box 1776, Williamsburg, VA 23187-1776; (757) 229-1000 www.colonialwilliamsburg.com; www.history.org/almanack/places/hb/hbcap.cfm

Restored capitol at Colonial Williamsburg , Virginia

> *At the turn of the twentieth century, Williamsburg was not what the visitor sees today. It was an old and decrepit farm town. When John D. Rockefeller visited in 1926 for a meeting of the Phi Beta Kappa Society at the College of William & Mary, he saw the town as a great historical memorial for those who had lived and struggled here in the founding of the nation. For the story of its restoration, see, http://www.history.org/foundation/journal/winter00_01/vision.cfm*

The delegates wished a "restoration of union and harmony," and reaffirmed that the "foundation of English liberty, and of all free government is a right in the people to participate in their legislative counsel." Since the colonies could not participate in Parliament "they are entitled to a free and exclusive power of legislation in their several provincial legislatures where their right of representation can alone be preserved, in all cases of taxation and internal polity..."

Declaration and Resolves. Next came the Declaration and Resolves, passed by the Continental Congress on October 14, which declared the Coercive Acts and the Quebec Act unconstitutional. It asserted that only the colonial legislatures had the authority for internal taxation.

The Articles of Association, using a Virginia Association model, quickly followed on October 20, which banned the importation of British goods and the slave trade. The message to King George III was that American goods would not be sold to England and Americans would not consume British goods until the Intolerable Acts were repealed.

The Congress then resolved to meet the following year if the King failed to cure the grievances of the colonies. This was the first time Americans had joined together outside the framework of the colonial governments established by England. Their spirit reflected the symbol that would later be on the great seal of the United States, the eagle with the sword of war in one claw and the olive branch of peace in the other.

Liberty or Death

In Virginia, the dissolved House of Burgesses met away from the royal governor at *St. John's Episcopal Church* in Richmond. There, on March 23, 1775, George Washington and Thomas Jefferson heard Patrick Henry challenge the Second Virginia Convention in a phrase that rang throughout the colonies, "Give me liberty or give me death."

It had now moved beyond simply an argument over trade and taxes. Parliament wished to demonstrate its authority over the colonists. To do that, an example would be made of Boston, the most rebellious of the colonies. General Thomas Gage, who was the Governor of Massachusetts as well as the new military commander, marched out to seize the arms of the colonists at Concord. On April 19, 1775 his detachment ran into the Minutemen at Lexington Green and after killing eight colonists marched on to Concord.

Shot Heard Round the World

The Minutemen were ready and there by the rude bridge at Concord they fought back. The British wheeled about to retreat to Boston, but the word spread through the countryside. More colonists took up positions behind rocks and trees along the line of march and the British suffered terrible casualties during the long way back.

Overlooking Boston, the rebels dug into Breed's Hill, with a fall back position on Bunker Hill on Charleston Peninsula. Guns were posted to fire on British ships in the Boston Harbor. The British assaulted the hill - later called the battle of Bunker Hill. They paid a high cost in the lives of British soldiers, but pushed the colonists off and secured English control of the harbor.

Rebellion

Parliament and George III had ignored the message from the First Continental Congress so again the delegates convened in Philadelphia. The Second Continental Congress was in session when word came of the fierce battles at

St. John's Episcopal Church

The oldest church in Richmond is St. John's Episcopal Church, constructed in 1741 by Richard Randolph. It was here, on March 23, 1775, that Patrick Henry, standing in pew 47, challenged the Second Virginia Convention which included George Washington and Thomas Jefferson. "Is life so dear, or peace so sweet as to be purchased at the price of chains and slavery? Forbid it, almighty God! I know not what course others may take, but as for me, give me liberty or give me death." Later in 1781, English soldiers, under the traitor Benedict Arnold, used the church as a barracks.

Visitors: The church is open to visitors and pew 47 is marked. Tours of the grounds and a description of Henry's speech daily 10:00 a.m. to 4:00 p.m, Sunday 1:00 p.m. to 4:00 p.m. There are re-enactments of Henry's speech each Sunday at 1:15 p.m. Memorial Day through Labor Day. Gift shop open until 4:00 p.m.

Directions: St. John's is located on East Broad Street between 24th and 25th Streets in Richmond, Virginia. Broad Street is exit 74C from I-95 and 183A on I-64.

Contact: St. John's Episcopal Church, 2401 East Broad Street, Richmond, Virginia 23223; (804) 648-5015; www.historicstjohnschurch.org

Breed's Hill and Bunker Hill.

At this same time, Virginia governor Lord Dunmore sent British marines under cover of darkness to seize the gunpowder stored in the Magazine at Williamsburg. To the Virginians, this was proof that there was a royal plot to deny them rights they had long enjoyed as English citizens.

Suddenly, the Continental Congress was in charge of a war. In spite of his defeat at Fort Necessity, Washington's military reputation remained high and when he appeared at the Second Continental Congress in his Virginia militia uniform the delegates did not hesitate to send him to Boston to take command of the Continental Army.

George Washington accepted command of an army that did not yet exist. Later, the American militias around Boston would become the first of the "continental" troops.

Still, there were many loyalists to the crown not swept up by the fervor of the revolutionists. Even though George III had ignored the Declaration and Resolves of the previous year, the Continental Congress offered in July the Olive Branch Petition. Again, it promised the continued loyalty of the people if the king would stop hostilities.

George III did not see the Olive Branch Petition and reconciliation did not happen. He chose to ignore the resistance to Parliament that was building in the colonies and on August 23, 1775, he issued a Proclamation for Suppressing Rebellion and Sedition, declaring the colonies in "open and avowed rebellion."

George III ascended the throne in 1760 and died in 1820. His stout defense of England during the Revolution and in the ensuing wars with France made him popular with the English people. He was learned and cultured, but during the last 11 years of his reign, he was disabled by a mental condition and Great Britain was ruled by the Prince Regent, later George IV.

GEORGE WASHINGTON

The First President

Birthplace: Pope's Creek

Date of Birth: February 22, 1732

Term: April 30, 1789 - March 3, 1797

Vice President: John Adams

1789-1797

Date of Death: December 14, 1799

Burial Place: Mount Vernon

Once the Continental Congress made the decision to send troops to aid the patriots in Boston, there was little hesitation in selecting the commander. He would leave his country two great gifts – the supremacy of civilian control over the military and the accountability of the president to the people. That lay in the future. He could not know of the ordeal ahead, nor could the delegates to the Second Continental Congress know that they had picked the indispensable man.

Early Years

George Washington was born on *Popes Creek* in Westmoreland County, Virginia, on February 22, 1732. Although his great grandfather had come to America in 1657, Washington's father, Augustine, was taken back to England by his mother. When she died, Augustine returned to America to the estate that his father and grandfather had created. His first wife died leaving him with three small children. He married his second wife Mary Ball in 1731, and the oldest of the five children of this marriage was George Washington.

Popes Creek
George Washington Birthplace

George Washington was born on February 22, 1732 on Popes Creek in Westmoreland County, Virginia, the son of Augustine Washington and Mary Ball. Washington lived here until he was three and a half years old. The house first passed to Washington's half-brother and then to his nephew, William Augustine Washington, who began to refer to it as "Wakefield." The original house was burned on Christmas Day 1779, and was never rebuilt. A middle-sized plantation manor house was reconstructed in 1930. It is not a replica of the birthplace house but a typical house of the upper classes of the period. In 1936, the foundations of the birth place house were uncovered a short distance from the memorial house. The Washington family burial ground has been identified and restored. At the entrance to the historic area is a replica of the Washington Monument. The property was first acquired in 1858 by the Commonwealth of Virginia and was later authorized as a national monument by Congress in 1930. It was opened to the public in 1932 on the 200th anniversary of Washington's birth. In addition to the birthplace home and burial ground, there is a film, *A Childhood Place,* and the historic area includes hiking trails, beach and picnic areas. It is administered by the National Park Service.

Visitors: The property is open every day except New Year's Day, Thanksgiving Day and Christmas Day from 9:00 a.m. to 5:00 p.m.

Directions: The birthplace is east from Fredericksburg about 38 miles on Virginia Route 3 and then north on Virginia Route 204.

Contact: George Washington Birthplace National Monument, 1732 Popes Creek Road, Washington's Birthplace, VA 22443-5115; (804) 224-1732; www.nps.gov/gewa

When Washington was three and half years old, his father moved the family from Popes Creek to a place on the Potomac called Little Hunting Creek. George lived there until he was six when his father moved the family to *Ferry Farm,* on the Rappahannock River across from Fredericksburg. Augustine Washington died in 1743 when George was eleven years old. His half-brother Lawrence inherited Little

Ferry Farm
Washington Boyhood Home

Ferry Farm was the place Washington referred to as "the home of my growing infancy..." His father Augustine moved the family here in 1738 when George was six years old. His father died when George was eleven and he lived here with his mother until he was sixteen, although he was often away visiting his two older half-brothers. It was called Ferry Farm because it was near the landing for the ferry from Stafford County to Fredericksburg. This was the place where legend has him throwing the silver dollar across the Rappahannock River and cutting down the cherry tree. No buildings survive from Washington's time there, but archeological excavations have located the original site of the house. Washington inherited the farm on his father's death and later sold it in 1772. In the 1980's it was donated by the Warren family as a memorial to Washington. Ferry Farm is owned and operated by The George Washington Foundation.

Visitors: Open daily to the public March through December from 10:00 a.m. to 4:00 p.m. Closed January and February except February 15 & 17. Self guided tours only. Group tours by reservation.

Directions: Go east from Fredericksburg on William Street (Virginia Route 3) and cross Rappahannock River on the Chatham Bridge, and turn right on Route 3, go to third stoplight, Ferry Farm is on the right.

Contact: George Washington's Ferry Farm, 268 Kings Highway, Fredericksburg, VA 22405; (540) 370-0732; http://www.kenmore.org/ff_home.html

Hunting Creek, his half-brother Augustine inherited the original family estate at Popes Creek and on his majority, Ferry Farm passed to George Washington.

Youth on the Frontier

After his father's death, George remained under the care of his mother, but spent a great amount of his time with his two older half-brothers, to the extent that he considered as his own home the estate that Lawrence created at Little Hunting Creek. Lawrence erected a plain mansion house on a high point on the Potomac shore. He named it in honor of Edward Vernon, his commander in the expedition to Cartagena when Lawrence was a British army officer.

Lawrence married Anne Fairfax, whose family home was at Belvoir, on the Potomac, now the site of the Army base. Belvoir burned to the ground in 1774 and the site was unoccupied until it was taken over by the War Department in 1912. Anne's father and the owner of Belvoir, William Fairfax, took an interest in the young George Washington who had recently begun a career as a surveyor and had helped lay out the streets of the new city, Alexandria.

Fairfax agreed to employ the sixteen year old Washington on a crew to survey the Fairfax lands in the Shenandoah Valley. This gave Washington his first look at Frederick Town, renamed Winchester in 1752.

Washington returned to take his test for a surveying license at the College of William & Mary which he received in 1749. Over the next four years he spent spring and fall surveying around Frederick Town.

Lawrence Washington became ill in 1751 and traveled to Barbados for a better climate. He took as a companion his 20 year old half-brother. It was the only time George Washington would leave the United States.

However, Lawrence did not improve and the following spring he returned to die and *Mount Vernon*, his home at Little Hunting Creek, passed to his wife and young daughter.

Political Beginning

George Washington's conduct in the defeats at Fort Necessity and with General Braddock in 1755 at Fort Duquesne was viewed favorably in the other colonies. Governor Dinwiddie rewarded him with a promotion to colonel in the Virginia militia. As the French and Indian War flared up on the Virginia frontier, Dinwiddie sent Washington to protect the settlers.

For the next three years *Washington's headquarters* were at Winchester. He constructed forts in Hampshire and Halifax counties and drew the plans and supervised the construction of Fort Loudoun in Winchester. His final contribu-

The Story Of Mount Vernon

Mount Vernon was first acquired by George Washington's great grandfather in 1674 and was known as the Little Hunting Creek Plantation. It was inherited by Lawrence Washington, George Washington's older half brother, who built the central two story portion. He named the property "Mount Vernon" in honor of Admiral Edward Vernon, the leader of a military expedition to Cartagena in which Lawrence had participated. At Lawrence's death, the property passed to his daughter, but the young girl soon died and George Washington inherited the property in 1754. He was able to lease the life estate interest of Lawrence's widow and by 1761 he had clear title. The house is located on Mansion House Farm, on a point where the Potomac turns toward the Chesapeake Bay. The four outlying farms are River Farm, Union Farm, Dogue Run Farm, and Muddy Hole Farm. Washington's will left a life estate to his wife, Martha, and on her death in 1802, Mount Vernon passed to Washington's nephew Bushrod Washington. It remained in the Washington family until the early 1850's when it was in a state of ruin. At that time, Ann Pamela Cunningham organized the Mount Vernon Ladies' Association and launched a fund raising campaign for the purchase and preservation of the estate. The Virginia General Assembly granted a charter to the new corporation and agreed to assume ownership of the property in the event the Association ever disbanded. On George Washington's birthday in February 1860, the Association took possession and to this day continues to own and maintain the house and grounds. Both George and Martha are buried on the grounds of Mount Vernon in the Washington Family Vault.

Visitors: Guided tours are provided for the mansion, but the grounds and many of the out buildings are self-guided. Mount Vernon is open every day of the year, but opening times may vary from 8:00 a.m. to 9:00 a.m. depending on the season. It has two gift shops and a large book selection. The third floor bedroom area is only open during the Christmas season.

Directions: From Alexandria, follow Washington Street south onto the Mount Vernon Memorial Highway which runs along the Potomac River. It can also be visited by boat (202) 554-8000 and bus (202) 637-7000. From I-95, take exit 166 east (Fairfax County Parkway) to Virginia Route 1, then north to Virginia Route 235.

Contact: Mount Vernon, 5514 Mount Vernon Memorial Highway, Mount Vernon, Virginia 22121; (703)780-2000; www.MountVernon.org

Mount Vernon, the most famous home in America, preserves the timeless story of George Washington. Shown is the east elevation (or the rear of the house) overlooking the Potomac River

Washington's Headquarters

George Washington first came to Winchester in 1749 as part of a crew surveying the lands of William Fairfax. Later, he returned in 1755 as a colonel in the Virginia Militia with the task of constructing forts along the Virginia frontier. The log and stone building at Braddock and Cork Streets was probably used as Washington's Headquarters. The building is now a museum which traces Washington's years in Winchester until 1758 when he returned to Mount Vernon.

Visitors: The sites in Winchester related to George Washington can be walked or driven. Maps and memorabilia are available at the Visitor Center.

Directions: Winchester lies in the lower Shenandoah Valley and can be reached from I-81 or I-66.

Contact: Winchester-Frederick County Visitor Center, 1360 Pleasant Valley Road, Winchester, Virginia 22601; (540) 542-1326, (800) 662-1360; http://www.visitwinchesterva.com/tours-and-itineraries/138-french-and-indian-war-foundation

tion just before he left the frontier was to participate in the successful campaign by General John Forbes against the French at Fort Duquesne.

Washington's political career began in Winchester when he ran for one of the two seats in the Virginia House of Burgesses for Frederick County. He lost that first election in 1755 but won in 1758 and again in 1761 after returning to Mount Vernon. He was elected from Fairfax when a seat became open in 1765. He remained in the House of Burgesses until he accepted command of the Continental Army in 1775.

Marriage of Washington

In 1759, Washington left the militia and returned to Mount Vernon to marry Martha Dandridge Custis. She was the young widow of Daniel Parke Custis and now one of the wealthiest women in Virginia. Through this marriage, Washington's moved into the state's most influential circles.

She had given birth to four children during her marriage to Custis, but only two survived. Washington raised them as his own. When the son, John Parke Custis, died from a fever following the Battle of Yorktown, Washington "adopted" the two youngest of his four children, Eleanor "Nelly" Custis and George Washington Parke Custis. Washington and Martha were not to have children of their own.

When Nelly married, George Washington bequeathed to her in his will the land on which the estate of *Woodlawn* was built. G. W. P. Custis built the estate he called Arlington which passed to his daughter Mary Anna Randolph Custis. She became the wife of Robert E. Lee, and during the Civil War, the estate was used as a burial ground for Union soldiers. It is now part of Arlington National Cemetery.

Washington the Farmer

During the fifteen years before the Revolutionary War, Washington was one of Virginia's most successful farmers. His innovations in crop diversification and farming techniques became a model for others. He acquired over 8,000 acres made up of five farms including *River Farm*. As with all large estates in Virginia at the time, the operation of Mount Vernon was based on slave labor.

Tobacco was the crop that had created the great estates of tidewater Virginia, but tobacco exhausted the soil. Many tobacco growers needed credit from year to year and they looked to English tobacco merchants for credit until the crop was sold. Under the trade laws imposed by England, the colonists sent all raw materials to England and bought manufactured goods only from England. This system created heavy debt throughout the colonies to English creditors with little hope it could ever be paid off.

Washington tried to free his estates from tobacco as early as 1764 by turning to wheat as a cash commodity. He

---

Woodlawn

This imposing brick house was built on 2000 acres of land bequeathed in his will by George Washington to Eleanor "Nelly" Custis and her new husband, Lawrence Lewis. It has long been called a wedding gift. Major Lawrence Lewis was Washington's nephew, the son of Betty Lewis of Historic Kenwood. Nelly and Lawrence Lewis constructed Woodlawn in 1802. Set on a prominent rise, the house looks to the Potomac River. Designed by William Thornton, architect of the U. S. Capitol, the early Federal style shows the influence of Historic Kenwood and the palladium features favored by Jefferson. The home is now owned by the National Trust for Historic Preservation.

Visitors: Guided tours daily March through November, from 12:00 p.m. to 4:00 p.m., but closed on Thanksgiving Day, and during the months of December, January and February, except President's Day. Nice colonial gift shop.

Directions: From Alexandria, south on Virginia Route 1 to the intersection with Virginia Route 235. From Mount Vernon, go south 2.8 miles on Virginia Route 235. From I-95, take exit 166 east on Virginia Route 286 (Fairfax County Parkway) to Virginia Route 1, then north to Virginia Route 235.

Contact: Woodlawn, 9000 Richmond Highway, Alexandria, Virginia 22309; (703) 780-4000; http://www.woodlawnpopeleighey.org/woodlawn

River Farm

William Clifton obtained ownership through marriage of 1,800 acres which he called Clifton's Neck. A public ferry from the property to Broad Creek in Maryland was part of the King's Highway. In 1760, George Washington purchased the property and renamed it River Farm. It was the northernmost parcel of Washington's five farms. He leased it out and received his rent in tobacco. Washington provided in his will for his secretary Tobias Lear to have a life estate in the property. In 1859, what remained of the original tract passed out of the Washington family. The house presently on the property was constructed in 1919 and was purchased along with a twenty-five acre parcel by the American Horticultural Society in 1973. The name of River Farm was restored to preserve Washington's reputation as a gardener and horticulturist. The Kentucky coffee tree was grown from seeds brought back by Washington from the Ohio valley. Two large black walnut trees are believed to have been on the property when Washington owned it. The Osage Orange is believed to have grown from seedlings Thomas Jefferson obtained from the Lewis and Clark expedition. The property is now the headquarters of the American Horticultural Society.

Visitors: Open daily Monday through Friday from 9:00 a.m. to 5:00 p.m., also on Saturdays from 9:00 a.m. to 1:00 p.m. from April through September. Closed on national holidays. Garden shop open Tuesday, Wednesday and Thursday 11:00 a.m. to 2:00 p.m.

Directions: River Farm is off the Mount Vernon Memorial Highway, 5 miles south of Alexandria, approximately halfway to Mount Vernon. Turn left on East Boulevard Drive.

Contact: Headquarters of the American Horticultural Society, 7931 East Boulevard Drive, Alexandria, Virginia 22308; (703) 768-5700 or (800) 777-7931; http://www.ahs.org/about-river-farm/history

built a *Grist Mill* in 1771 and not only sold the flour but charged a fee for others to use the mill. On the same site he built a distillery. He also took large quantities of fish from the Potomac which was an important food source for the slaves. Shortly after he became president, he constructed a threshing barn for the wheat - Washington's famous "round" or sixteen sided barn.

Washington's Grist Mill and Distillery

George Washington wanted to make Mount Vernon less dependent on tobacco. He put his fields into wheat and in the early 1770's constructed a new grist mill on Dogue Run. It replaced an early mill which had deteriorated and was no longer efficient. Special buhr millstones imported from France ground a high quality flour for the new mill which Washington exported. The containers were loaded on flat bottom boats and floated down Dogue Run to a dock on the Potomac. Washington also sold his flour locally, and the mill became a market where other farmers could sell their wheat or have it milled for their own use. About 1791, Washington installed a more efficient system of moving the heavy barrels of grain through the milling process. The state of Virginia reconstructed the mill in 1933 and ran it as a state park. Mount Vernon Estate and Gardens then took over the mill in 1996. After five years of research, it was reconstructed to the same specifications and system used by Washington. The water-powered mill is fully operational and millers will demonstrate the colonial milling process. Washington also built a distillery on the site of the Grist Mill which was in operation several years before his death. The building eventually disappeared but archeologists uncovered the foundations and reconstructed the distillery. Visitors can observe the whiskey-making process.

Visitors: Washington's Grist Mill and Distillery is open daily April through October from 10:00 a.m. to 5:00 p.m. There is a small gift shop where corn meal, flour and whiskey produced on the site may be purchased.

Directions: At the intersection of Virginia Routes 1 and 235, near Woodlawn. It is 2.8 miles from Mount Vernon. From I-95, take exit 163, go north 3.5 miles on Virginia Route 1 to intersection with Route 235.

Contact: Mount Vernon Estates and Gardens, Mount Vernon, Virginia 22121; (703)780-3383; Gift shop (703) 360-1750; http://www.mountvernon.org/gristmill; http://www.mountvernon.org/distillery

Washington as Entrepreneur

Washington's passion to own land began when he was just sixteen. While surveying for Lord Fairfax, he purchased about 500 acres. When he was stationed at Winchester he bought two lots and would eventually own over 3000 acres in western Virginia. Washington had a strong belief that Virginia's colonists would spread west. His land holdings grew to include almost 10,000 acres near the Ohio River, over 20,000 acres along the Kanawha River, and 3,000 acres in the Northwest Territory. He held an additional 7,500 acres in other states.

The potential wealth of his land holdings made him an early advocate of building a canal along the Potomac to open trade with the Ohio Valley. The project came to life after the Revolutionary War when Washington hosted a meeting at Mount Vernon. This led to the *Patowmack Canal* around Great Falls, a miraculous engineering effort for early 19th century technology. Washington did not live to see the project finished in 1802 but it was in operation until 1830 when the Chesapeake and Ohio Canal made it obsolete.

After his return to Mount Vernon from the French and Indian War, Washington became interested in the *Great Dismal Swamp*. With other investors he purchased 40,000 acres and dug the Washington Ditch to drain the swamp in the hopes of turning it into farmland. When the project failed, Washington became pessimistic about the future of this enterprise and tried unsuccessfully to sell his interest.

Washington the Son

George Washington was eleven years old when his father died. His half-brother Lawrence Washington appears to have been a father substitute and encouraged him to become a midshipman in the English navy. George was only fourteen and his mother would not consent. He left his mother's control when he was sixteen and went to the frontier to survey for Lord Fairfax.

What affection there may have been between Washington and his mother is not clear. Although she complained of not having money, Washington cared for her after he re-

Patowmack Canal

It was the result of Washington's vision to use the Potomac River as the means to open the Ohio River valley for development. He assembled representatives in 1785 from Maryland and Virginia to form the Mount Vernon Compact. It was an agreement to use the Potomac River as a "common highway" to the west. The Patowmack Company was created with Washington as the first president. Its task was to build canals around the obstructions in the river which prevented the passage of the boats, such as water falls or rock formations. There were five separate places where canals were necessary, but the greatest achievement was the Patowmack Canal around the Great Falls, 1200 yards long with locks dropping the barges seventy-five feet at the lower end. Washington did not live to see it completed in 1802, but it operated for over twenty-five years before it was taken over by the new Chesapeake and Ohio Canal Company. Great Falls Park is managed by the National Park Service.

Visitors: Open every day except Christmas. The park is closed at dark and gates are locked. There is a Visitor Center with exhibits on the development of the canal. Guided programs year-round.

Directions: The park entrance is on Virginia Route 193 halfway between I-495 and Virginia Route 7.

Contact: Great Falls Park, The National Park Service, George Washington Memorial Parkway, Turkey Run Park, McLean, Virginia 22101; (703) 285-2964; www.nps.gov/grfa

ceived his inheritance. In 1772, he purchased a house for her in Fredericksburg - now, the *Mary Washington House.* This placed her close to *Historic Kenmore,* the home of Washington's sister, Betty Lewis.

Washington Takes Command

When the Second Continental Congress convened at Philadelphia in May, 1775, they learned of the battle at Bunker Hill. Feelings ran high to help the patriots who now had the Redcoats in Boston under siege. The Congress turned to one of its members, a delegate from Virginia, wearing the uniform of his state's militia. They made him a commander and he rode north to Boston to find his army.

Washington did not believe it was the wish of the

Great Dismal Swamp

The Great Dismal Swamp stretches across the Virginia-North Carolina border, thousands of years old and once 2,200 miles square. George Washington saw the Great Dismal Swamp in 1763, and intrigued by its beauty and commercial potential convinced a group of investors to buy 40,000 acres. Their plan was to drain the swamp and turn it into farmland. Slave labor cut two canals, the five mile Washington Ditch and the Jericho Ditch, to drain into Lake Drummond at the center of the Swamp. This effort did not work but the two ditches did provide a means of floating timber out. Two hundred years later, Union Camp harvested the last of the virgin forest and donated 49,100 acres as a wildlife refuge. With the purchase of additional acreage, the Great Dismal Swamp Wildlife Refuge of 107,100 acres was established in 1974. It is managed by the Department of the Interior. Washington was also part of an enterprise to build a canal which took twelve years to dig by hand. This was started in 1784, but before his death Washington lost faith in the venture. However, by 1805, the Dismal Swamp Canal was in use and throughout the 1800's was an important commercial operation. In 1929, it was sold to the Federal Government and is now operated by the Army Corps of Engineers. Today, it is a part of the Atlantic Intercoastal Waterway.

Visitors: Open daily from sunrise to sunset, there are many trails open to hiking and biking. A boardwalk trail begins at the Washington Ditch entrance through the Swamp for about one mile. Boating and fishing year round on Lake Drummond. The Refuge Office is open Monday - Friday from 8:00 a.m. to 4:00 p.m. Closed all Federal holidays.

Directions: From I-64, follow signs to Suffolk. Exit at 58/460/13. Pass Hampton Roads Airport. Take downtown Suffolk exit. Left at 6th light onto Main Street/Route 32 south. Follow 32 south out of town. Take a left to stay on 32 south. Left on Cypress Chapel Road (Route 675), left on White Marsh Road (Route 642). At four way stop, straight to Washington Ditch and Jericho Lane entrances. From the same four way stop, take a right on Desert Road. (Route 604) to go to office.

Contact: Refuge Manager, Great Dismal Swamp National Wildlife Refuge, 3100 Desert Road, Suffolk, Virginia 23434; (757) 986-3705; http://www.fws.gov/refuge/great_dismal_swamp/; NC Dismal Swamp Canal Visitor Center, 2356 US Highway 17 N., South Mills, North Carolina 27976-9425; (252) 771-8333 colonies to "set up for independency." He also admonished Great Britain that none would submit to the loss of those rights "essential to the happiness of every free state." By November, 1775, it was clear King George III would use military might to force political control on rebellious British America.

A small Continental force moved to secure the northern colonies by campaigns against Montreal and Quebec. A daring expedition to Quebec, through unmapped territory, led by Benedict Arnold, was caught by winter and almost broke apart. Arnold finally reached Quebec and launched an unsuccessful assault at great loss of life. The Americans went into a winter siege around the city.

When spring 1776 arrived, Arnold decided he could

Mary Washington House

George Washington bought a small frame house in Fredericksburg for his mother, Mary Ball Washington, in 1772. Mary Washington at first resisted leaving Ferry Farm, but was contented to live here for seventeen years until her death. Washington added onto the original section of the house built about 1760. The property was acquired in 1890 by the Association for the Preservation of Virginia Antiquities which restored the house and gardens. It is now owned and operated by Washington Heritage Museums. Mary Washington's grave site is located nearby at the intersection of Washington Avenue and Pitt Street.

Visitors: The house is open from March 1 through October, Monday to Saturday, from 11:00 a.m. to 5:00 p.m. and Sunday from 12:00 noon to 4:00 p.m.; November 1 through February, Monday to Saturday from 11:00 a.m. to 4:00 p.m. and Sunday from 12:00 noon to 4:00 p.m. The house is closed Thanksgiving Day, December 24, 25, 31 and New Year's Day. There is a gift shop.

Directions: Fredericksburg can be reached from I-95 or Virginia State Route 1. The Mary Washington House is on the corner of Charles Street and Lewis Street.

Contact: Mary Washington House, Washington Heritage Museum, 1200 Charles Street, Fredericksburg, Virginia 22401; (540) 373-1569; http://www.washingtonheritagemuseums.org/

not hold Quebec and retreated to Fort Ticonderoga. At the same time, the British evacuated Boston. General William Howe realized that George Washington, now in command of the American Forces, was trying to bring Boston Port under the range of heavy artillery.

War in the North

When the British left Boston, Washington followed. Secure in New York, General William Howe offered to cease hostilities if the Americans would repudiate the Declaration of Independence. When Washington refused, Howe attacked and Washington retreated to Brooklyn Heights on Long Island. After several sharp engagements, Washington moved to New Jersey closely tracked by Lord Charles Cornwallis. Slowly, Washington's army began to evaporate as the militia enlistments expired and men deserted.

Winter sent the British army into camp and Washington took the opportunity for a bold move across the Delaware River on Christmas eve. By dawn, he had his small army in position near Trenton, which was defended by Hessian troops. Caught completely by surprise, the Hessian commander was killed and his troops gave up. Cornwallis moved quickly to retaliate. When his scouts saw the American camp fires, Cornwallis readied for a dawn attack. Tricked by Washington, he found the fires were a decoy and that the Americans had slipped around to the British rear at Princeton.

Defeat of the British at Trenton and Princeton was decisive. Washington had restored the belief that victory over the greatest military power in the world might still be achieved. Authenticated copies of the Declaration of Independence were sent by the Continental Congress to each of the new "United States."

In 1777, the British launched two offensives against the colonists. In New York, the English General "Gentleman Johnny" Burgoyne captured Fort Ticonderoga, and in October, marched on Saratoga. There, under Horatio Gates, the Americans won a decisive victory, lifting the spirit of the colonists.

As winter approached, Howe took Philadelphia and chased the Continental Congress to Lancaster and then to York. The British soundly punished the Continental Army at Brandywine Creek and Germantown before George Washington moved his soldiers into winter quarters at Valley Forge.

Valley Forge

Described by Washington as "barefoot and otherwise naked," without blankets, the army suffered terribly during the long winter months, decimated by sickness and desertion.

On the memorial arch at Valley Forge this inscription appears:

"...and here in this place of sacrifice, in this vale of humiliation, in this valley of the shadow of that death out of which the life of America rose regenerate and free let us resolve with an abiding faith that to them Union would seem as dear, and liberty as sweet, and progress as glorious, as they were to our Fathers and are to you and me, and that the Institutions which have made us happy, preserved by the virtue of our children shall bless the remotest generation of the time to come."

It was not until Valley Forge that the Americans would be drilled into a real army under the direction of Frederick Wilhelm von Steuben, a German soldier of fortune. They were always a partisan group, farmers and shopkeepers, citizen soldiers. They could not be commanded in the military tradition of complete control and obedience, but they could be led. In Washington, resolute and courageous, they found a natural leader for an army of free men.

Conway Cabal

George Washington had earned the loyalty of his officers and men but not all members of the Continental Congress were supporters. Because of the spectacular victory of Gates at Saratoga, some proposed that he replace Washington. Thomas Conway, one of the French volunteers, fighting with the colonists, wrote a letter critical of Washington.

This incident has been referred to as the Conway Cabal, but there is little evidence that an organized effort was ever made to depose Washington. Conway was seriously wounded in a duel when a young officer on Washington's staff took offense. Still, the criticism continued from some members of Congress to add to the misery of the winter at Valley Forge.

French Alliance

Because of the desperate condition of the army at Valley Forge, the French were concerned that the Continental Congress might negotiate a settlement of the conflict that would return the colonies to British control. In the only alliance with a foreign power until World War I, America and France concluded the Alliance of 1778. This would bring the support of the French navy under Admiral Françoise de Grasse and the army under Comte de Rouchambeau. The aid of France would prove decisive in the eventual American victory.

In the spring of 1778, Henry Clinton replaced General Howe. Clinton decided to pull back from Philadelphia to New York. Washington ordered General Charles Lee to strike him on the line of march at Monmouth, New Jersey, but Lee failed to press the attack and the British were able to fight their way into New York.

However, they had run out of room to maneuver. They were now forced into a pocket and held at bay by the Continental Army. Washington devised a strategy to move the war south.

War in the South

The British had captured Savannah in 1778 and used it as a base of operations to move a force under General Clinton against Charleston. The city surrendered in February, 1780, in a major victory for Great Britain. The Americans struck back with a guerilla war, vicious and bitter on both sides. The Continental Congress sent a force under Horatio Gates, the victor of Saratoga. Then, in August, Lord Cornwallis demolished the Americans and Gates' career at Camden, South Carolina.

Two months later an army of colonists loyal to the King suffered a stinging defeat by patriot militia at Kings Mountain, North Carolina. George Washington sent Nathaniel Greene to take charge. In an unusual maneuver, Greene divided his army into two wings. Cornwallis sent Banastre Tarleton against the wing commanded by Daniel Morgan. The British attacked at Cowpens in January 1781, but the fire of Morgan's militia broke the charge and Tarleton withdrew.

Greene moved north to get reinforcements, but Lord Cornwallis was relentless in the pursuit. The armies finally closed at Guilford Courthouse in March. Casualties were about the same on both sides when Greene withdrew from the field. Cornwallis regrouped at Wilmington and then devised a strategy that set him on the road to Yorktown.

Cornwallis moved inland, apparently in an effort to raise support from loyalists, but this put his army far from the coast where they could be supplied. He ran into a small force of 2,500 regular troops at Richmond under the **Marquis de Lafayette.** The Americans continued to move away rather than confront the British army of 7,500 men.

Victory at Yorktown

General Clinton ordered Cornwallis to move to the coast where the British fleet could take his army to Charleston or to New York. Cornwallis moved down the Virginia peninsula between the York and James Rivers, shadowed by Lafayette. Cornwallis occupied the port of **Yorktown,** only 20 miles from where the first English settlement in America was established at Jamestown.

In the meantime, Washington faked an attack on Staten Island to mask his intentions and moved his troops by transport down Chesapeake Bay. A French fleet under Admiral de Grasse arrived from the West Indies and entered the Virginia Capes. It landed troops to reinforce Lafayette. The Redcoats were bottled up in Yorktown and waited for their fleet to remove them.

Cornwallis' rescue was not to be. The British ships found their entrance to the Bay blocked between Cape Henry and Cape Charles by de Grasse. With no escape by sea and his position surrounded on land, Cornwallis surrendered on October 17, 1781.

After the battle of Yorktown, England's prime minister North said, "It is over." Two years later in September 1783, the Treaty of Paris (Peace Treaty of 1783) acknowledged that all the land from the Atlantic to the Mississippi was in the new United States of America

Yorktown Victory Center

Yorktown Victory Center was built in 1976 for the Bicentennial. The exhibits trace America's colonial history to its emergence as a new nation after the Revolutionary War. An open air exhibit marks the events that led to the Declaration of Independence. Inside the museum there are "witnesses to revolution," historical interpreters who tell the story of the long struggle for independence. An 18 minute film, "A Time of Revolution," is shown every half hour. Upon exiting, there is a Continental Army encampment and historical interpreters talk about their daily lives as soldiers. A typical 18th century farm demonstrates how Virginians lived after the Revolution. The Yorktown Victory Center, west of Yorktown, is operated by the Jamestown-Yorktown Foundation. The Visitors Center and Battlefield is east of Yorktown.

Visitors: A visit to Yorktown should begin at the Yorktown Victory Center, which is open daily from 9:00 a.m. to 5:00 p.m., all year except Christmas and New Year's Day.

Directions: From Williamsburg, take the Colonial Parkway to its terminus on the York River. From I-64 take exit 242 east and follow signs to Yorktown. From Virginia Route 17, south or north, watch for signs to Yorktown.

Contact: Yorktown Victory Center, 200 Water St., Yorktown, VA 23690; (757) 887-1776; www.historyisfun.org

Yorktown Visitor Center and Battlefield

A tour of the battlefield should starts with a 16 minute film, "Siege at Yorktown." There is also a book store and a museum of Revolutionary War artifacts. Park Rangers provide guided tours at the battlefield. Audio cassettes are available for self guided auto tours. Maps are provided for a walking tour of the town which includes the home of Thomas Nelson, a signer of the Declaration of Independence, who permitted his house to be shelled when it was discovered Cornwallis had set up a headquarters there. The Yorktown Visitors Center is operated by the National Park Service.

Visitors: Open daily 9:00 a.m. to 5:00 p.m. except Christmas Day and New Year's Day.

Directions: See directions to Yorktown Victory Center.

Contact: Colonial National Historical Park, P O Box 210, Yorktown, Virginia 23690; (757) 898-2410; www.nps.gov/york/

Marquis de la Fayette

Christened Marie Joseph Paul Yves Roch Gilbert du Motier, he inherited his family's fortune at eleven years old and became the Marquis de la Fayette. He was a captain in the French calvary when he became enthused with the colonists' fight for freedom. Barely twenty, he came to America in 1777 and offered his services without pay. The Continental Congress made him a major general and he fought at Brandywine, Monmouth and the campaign in Rhode Island. He returned home after the winter at Valley Forge and convinced the French government it was time to aid the colonists. France sent money and troops under Comte de Rouchambeau. Lafayette returned and helped trap Cornwallis at Yorktown.

In the early days of the French Revolution, Lafayette supported reform. Like many aristocrats during the "reign of terror," he was imprisoned and his wife's family went to the guillotine. His wife, Adrienne Lafayette, may have been saved by the intervention of Elizabeth Monroe. James Monroe, then minister to France, removed Lafayette's son from danger by granting him a passport to America. Named for George Washington, the young boy lived for more than a year at Mount Vernon.

In 1824, Lafayette visited America at the invitation of President Monroe. He returned to great acclaim and was the first foreigner to address both houses of Congress. His grand tour included all 25 states and in Charlottesville he dined with Thomas Jefferson and James Madison. He was deeply in debt and a grateful America gave him $200,000 and a township in Florida. He died in 1834 and dirt from Bunker Hill was spread over his grave in the Picpus cemetery in Paris. In 1917, when the American Doughboys came to aid the French in World War I, the parade ended at Lafayette's tomb where the speaker declared, "Lafayette, we are here!" In 2002, the U. S. Congress made him an honorary American citizen, "forever a symbol of freedom."

Civilian Control of the Military

The most momentous contribution Washington made as a soldier came following the end of the war. Within four years after the bitter winter at Valley Forge, he was the head of a conquering army. His popularity in every area of society was enormous. However, his officers were bitter toward

Congress, feeling it had failed them in the long struggle.

A Colonel Nicola wrote Washington that the country could not "become a nation under a Republican form of government." He proposed "the establishment of a kingdom," with Washington as the king.

Washington wrote back that "you could not have found a person to whom to your schemes are more disagreeable...let me conjure you then, if you have any regard for your country - concern for yourself or posterity - or respect for me, to banish these thoughts from your mind & never communicate, as from yourself or anyone else, a sentiment of the like nature."

Setting the Course

With many of the officers and men in debt, the personal affairs of almost all in ruin from the long absence from home, the army was on the verge of mutiny. Under the Articles of Confederation, adopted in 1781, the states did not give the Continental Congress the right of taxation. Many of the states refused to raise the sums necessary for the pay and bonuses due the officers and men of the Continental Army. The Federalists in the Congress were content to let the situation worsen because it supported their argument for a central taxing authority.

Finally, the army turned to Horatio Gates, hero of Saratoga, who set a meeting in Newburgh, N. Y. for March 15, 1783. Washington saw it as a challenge to the existence of the new country and, unannounced, strode into the room. He took some notes from his coat and placed on his spectacles, which he told the assembled men he needed, since he had gone "almost blind in the service of my country." When Washington finished his remarks there were tears in the eyes of many. It would be years before all would get their pay but the mutiny was over.

One of the great issues debated by the colonists before the Revolution was the right of a government to maintain standing armies. Armies ultimately became the balance of power to subjugate the citizenry and there was great concern during the war that Washington invoked such devotion from his men that he could become a dictator.

In an act that established the American tradition of civilian control over the military, Washington surrendered his sword to Congress and went home to Mount Vernon. When King George III heard that Washington had turned down a chance to establish a monarchy in the new nation, he is reported to have said, "If that is true Washington is the greatest man who ever lived."

Interlude at Mount Vernon

Washington now could devote attention to his fields and animals and great mansion house, to repair the neglect of the past eight years. He was 52 and assumed that the great adventures of his life were over.

He welcomed visitors and there were many; he sat for portraits; he engaged in correspondence; he was invited to visit other countries but always declined. He helped establish **Christ Church** in Alexandria since **Pohick Church,**

Christ Church

Historic Christ Church was completed in 1773. Washington had been a member of the parish since 1764, but was also a member of Truro Parish and most often attended **Pohick Church** in Fairfax. After 1783, when he returned from the Revolutionary War, until his death, he attended Christ Church. The interior of the church was restored in the 1890's to its original colonial style.

Visitors: Open to visitors Monday to Saturday from 9:00 a.m. to 4:00 p.m. and Sunday from 2:00 to 4:30 p.m. All visits are guided by a trained docent. For large groups please call (703) 549-2450.

Directions: Christ Church is in Alexandria at 118 North Washington Street at the intersection with Cameron Street. North Washington Street becomes Mount Vernon Memorial Highway south of the city.

Contact: Historic Christ Church. 118 N. Washington Street, Alexandria, Virginia 22314; (703) 549-1450; Gift shop (703) 836-5258; www.historicchristchurch.org/; Sunday from 8:45 a.m. to 2:00 p.m., Tuesday-Saturday from 10:00 a.m. to 4:00 p.m.

---

which he attended before the Revolution had fallen into disuse. He was visited by the Marquis de Lafayette, and when they parted it would be for the last time, but whose son, George Washington Lafayette, would seek refuge with Washington from the terror of French revolution.

Washington saw the country as a whole, not a group of states. He believed the country could never prosper until the issues of trade and taxes ignored state boundaries. A conference at Mount Vernon led to a call for delegates to a convention in Annapolis. Although the northern states did not show up, James Madison and Alexander Hamilton called for a Great Convention in Philadelphia to amend and correct the Articles of Confederation to enable the country to act with a central voice.

Washington was elected as president of what turned

Pohick Church

The original church, attended by George Washington from the early 1760's, was located several miles from the current Pohick Episcopal Church. Washington prepared a map with the location of all the parishioners to convince the members of the building committee that the location of the old church was not convenient. The decision was then made to build the church on the present site. It was not completed until 1773. Services were stopped in 1785 and the church was eventually abandoned. It was used again in the 1830's, but was damaged during the Civil War. In 1874, services were started again and in 1890 restoration began. Washington's pew is still identified for visitors. One of the occasional ministers at Pohick was Mason Weems who was Washington's earliest biographer. Among his many stories of Washington's childhood was the legend of the cherry tree.

Visitors: Open daily from 9:00 a.m. to 4:30 p.m. Brochures are available at the back of the church

Directions: Pohick Episcopal Church is located on Richmond Highway (Virginia Route 1) at Telegraph and Old Colchester Roads, Fairfax, Virginia, 6.2 miles from Mount Vernon. From I-95 take exit 163, go north on U.S. Route 1 for approximately 2 miles.

Contact: Historic Pohick Episcopal Church, 9301 Richmond Highway, Lorton, Virginia 22079; (703) 339-6572; www.pohick.org

into the Constitutional Convention of 1787. In the forming of the Constitution, many of the delegates may have felt that the office of President of the United States was created with the man already in mind.

The First President

The trip from Virginia to Washington's first inauguration in New York City was filled with adoring crowds and much pomp. There was even an effort to call Washington "His Highness, the President of the United States," so that the first President of the United States would not seem, by title, inferior to European royalty. Secure in himself and in the people of his country, Washington rejected any comparison to the practices of the monarchy. He saw the presidency as an extension of the people's will and rejected all efforts to upset that balance of power.

At the height of his authority, when the role of the presidency was still unformed, with no guide of conduct except his own vision, he gave it a direction that influenced the generations to come. He is the only president who received every vote in the electoral college, but after two terms, he again chose to return to the people the power to choose a new leader and retired to Mount Vernon. He understood, beyond those who invited him to greater prestige and power, the contribution he must make to that role in which a unique tide of political thought had placed him.

Selection of the Capital City

Washington was inaugurated in New York but the debate continued on the location of a permanent capital. Previously, Congress had met in Philadelphia, Baltimore, Lancaster, York, Princeton, Annapolis and Trenton; cities that were again considered. An agreement was engineered by Alexander Hamilton for the northern states to agree to place the capital on the Potomac in return for the southern states supporting Hamilton's plan for the federal government to assume the debts of the states from the Revolutionary War.

The final location of the capitol was left to Washington and he picked an area close to Alexandria carved from Maryland and Virginia divided by the Potomac River. It would carry his name, Washington, a daily reminder of the preeminent American, who became the *"Father of his country."*

Jefferson and Hamilton

The conflicts that had divided the delegates to the Constitutional Convention were mirrored in Washington's selection of Thomas Jefferson for Secretary of State and Alexander Hamilton for Secretary of the Treasury. Around these two men swirled the competing forces for direction of the new nation.

Hamilton had served on Washington's staff during the war and was a hero at the Battle of Yorktown and had been a delegate to the Constitutional Convention. He be-

---

"Father of his country"

It seems to have arisen during the Revolutionary War in the mind of the people that George Washington was the "father" of the new nation. An almanac published in 1778 in Lancaster, Pennsylvania has the figure of Fame on the cover holding a portrait of Washington. From her trumpet she sounded the words, "Des Landes Vater," or "father of the land." During the Revolutionary War, a French officer escorted Washington to Providence, Rhode Island. He later recorded that the people came out of their homes eager to greet Washington and addressed him as "father." The earliest biography of Washington, written eight years after his death, describes him on the occasion of his Farewell Address as the "father of the country." In his biography of Washington, John Marshall, an officer during the Revolutionary War, and later Chief Justice of the Supreme Court, quotes a letter written at the time of Washington's death. The letter was to John Adams and observed that the country "mourns a father." Some forty years after his great contribution to the American cause during the war, the Marquis de Lafayette returned to America. He visited the U. S. Military Academy at West Point. The school had been proposed by Washington and made official by Jefferson in his first term. On the wall of the reception hall the Marquis saw the portraits of Washington, Jefferson and then president John Quincy Adams. Under the Washington portrait was the title: "Father Of His Country."

---

lieved in a diversified economy, based on manufacturing and trade, supported by tariffs, and funded by a national bank. Hamilton favored life terms for the president and the Senate and wanted strong central control at the expense of state sovereignty.

Jefferson, the author of the Declaration of Independence, had not been at the Constitutional Convention. At that time, he was serving as Minister to France. Jefferson envisioned a more restrained central power as contemplated by the tenth amendment with an economy based on agriculture and a broad opportunity for all citizens to participate in government.

Hamiltonian ideas became the tenets of the Federalist party, eventually causing Jefferson to resign and return to Monticello.

Washington had struggled with the self-interest of the states and the lack of power in the Continental Congress to support the war. His belief that a central authority was necessary for the survival of the new nation led him to favor Hamilton.

Although Washington is often labeled a Federalist, political parties had not formed as they would later in Jefferson's election over John Adams in 1800. Generally referred to as anti-Federalists, Jeffersonian republicans criticized Washington during his second term for favoring national power at the expense of the states. Washington was undeterred from the course he had set and survives as a universal leader, the patriarch of a new nation struggling to find an identity.

Seeds of War

Shortly after Washington took office, unrest in France escalated into revolution. It veered out of control as a reign of terror brought scores of nobles and clergy, as well as Louis XVI and his queen, Marie Antoinette, to the guillotine. France tried to impart their revolution throughout Europe and sparked a war with England.

Loyalties in America were divided as Federalists supported Great Britain and republicans favored France, Washington followed a neutral course in order to keep the young country from another war. The conflict between France and England would go on for 22 years. Eventually, it would draw the United States into the War of 1812.

Farewell Address

Washington had wanted to return home at the end of his first term. He asked James Madison to draft for him a farewell speech. When the public learned Washington intended to leave the presidency, it was the universal reaction that the nation could not survive without him. There simply was no one to take his place.

Four years later, he would not be dissuaded. He pulled out Madison's draft and discussed his ideas for a final address with Alexander Hamilton. Washington then revised Hamilton's draft. This became Washington's Farewell Address, published in the *Philadelphia Advertiser* in September 1796. He reminded America that it was now "one people," and that all parts have a "particular interest in union." He warned against "passionate attachments" to other nations, either based on fondness or hatred. In public and in private affairs, he offered the maxim that "honesty is the best policy."

Death of Washington

Washington returned to Mount Vernon but not to a contented retirement. When it appeared a French invasion would drag America into the war between England and France, Washington agreed to lead the American forces. The constant attacks on him by the republicans ruptured his long friendship with Jefferson. There was much dissatisfaction with John Adams and there was hope that Washington would run again in 1800.

He attended a military review at *Gadsby's Tavern* in Alexandria in November, 1799. One month later death came to George Washington on December 14, 1799. Two days before he had toured his plantation on horseback in a cold wind laced with snow and hail. That evening he became hoarse and by the next afternoon he was in some distress.

Gadsby's Tavern Museum

Gadsby's Tavern was built soon after the new town of Alexandria was chartered in 1749. A license to operate an "ordinary," or "grog-shop" was issued for the property in 1756. The original building was removed and the Georgian style City Tavern was built in 1785 and the Federal-style City Hotel in 1792. They were leased to John Gadsby in 1796. A plaque on the building reads:

Gadsby Tavern

Erected 1792

Popular resort and famous hostelry

of the eighteenth century.

Here was held in 1798 the celebration of Washington's Birthday in which he participated, and from its steps Washington held his last military review and gave his last military order November 1799.

The Tavern and City Hotel continued to operate until the early 1900's when the Metropolitan Museum of Art in New York City bought the ballroom, the front door and a fireplace. A preservation movement saved the remainder of the building which is now owned and operated by the City of Alexandria. Both George Washington, the Marquis La Fayette and Thomas Jefferson visited here. For the history of the sale of the ballroom http://www.historicalexandriafoundation.org/preservation/gadsbys_tavern.aspx

Visitors: The Tavern is open for dining. Gadsby's Tavern Museum guided tours November through March, Wednesday to Saturday, from 11:00 a.m. to 4:00 p.m. and Sunday from 1:00 p.m. to 4:00 p.m.; from April through October, Tuesday to Saturday from 10:00 a.m. to 5:00 p.m. and Sunday - Monday from 1:00 p.m. to 5:00 p.m. Candlelight tours from 7:15 p.m. to 9:15 p.m.

Directions: In the center of Old Town Alexandria, at the corner of N. Royal and Cameron Streets.

Contact: Gadsby's Tavern Museum, 134 N. Royal St., Alexandria, VA 22314; (703) 746-4242; http://alexandriava.gov/GadsbysTavern; also http://www.gadsbystavernrestaurant.com/index.html

At that time, the doctors called it quinsy, which today would be diagnosed as "acute epiglottitis."

Early the next day, he was in extreme discomfort and messengers were sent for medical help. He asked Martha to get his will which he gave to her. The doctors tried to treat him with a mixture of vinegar and molasses and through the day they took blood from his arm. Blood letting was an acceptable medical practice at the time and each time it seemed to give Washington some comfort.

He was stoic as death approached as he had been through his life, finally telling the doctors not to take any more trouble, "but let me go off quietly. I cannot last long." He died about 11:30 that night in the presence of at least six persons, which included Martha Washington, Tobias Lear, his friend and secretary, his body servant Christopher, and three doctors. His last words were, "Tis well."

A memorial service was held at the **Presbyterian Meeting House** in Alexandria where the bells tolled for four days. He had requested in his will that he receive a private burial, but many citizens attended his funeral procession on December 18, 1799 at Mount Vernon.

He was buried with full military honors and Masonic rites were performed. He was placed in the old burial vault, but in 1831, his and Martha's bodies were moved to a new vault which was built at Mount Vernon as he requested in his will.

Washington's Will

George Washington began his **last will and testament**, "I, George Washington of Mount Vernon - a citizen of the United States." He made a number of specific bequests of money and personal items. The bulk of his property, including Mount Vernon, was left to Martha for her life. Martha occupied Mount Vernon until her death when it passed to the collateral heirs of Lawrence Washington.

George Washington provided in his will that his slaves would be freed on the death of his wife Martha. He delayed their freedom because he felt she needed the slaves

Old Presbyterian Meeting House

A brick sanctuary was first erected on the site in 1775 and completed in 1794. The manse at the rear of the church was built in 1787. George Washington had contributed to the original building fund and attended services in 1798. At his death memorial services were held here. The church's bell, the only one in Alexandria, rang four days and nights. When the congregation divided in 1817, it became the First Presbyterian Church. The interior of the building was destroyed by a bolt of lightning in 1835. A long effort to rebuild was ended by the Civil War and the church finally closed in 1889. A restoration effort was begun in 1925 which called the church the Old Presbyterian Meeting House, but it was not until 1949 that regular services began.

Visitors: Enter the church grounds from S. Royal Street and someone at the church office will open the church.

Directions: From Washington Street go east on King Street toward the Potomac River to S. Royal St., then south several blocks to 316.

Contact: Old Presbyterian Meeting House, Office at 316 South Royal St., Alexandria, VA 22314-3716; (703) 549-6670; http://www.opmh.org/

to run Mount Vernon. Martha had only a life estate interest in the slaves she inherited on the death of her first husband and these could not be freed by Washington. Several years after Washington's death, Martha freed the slaves left to her by Washington, but many of those in which she had only a life estate continued in slavery after her death.

His Country Remembers

Washington led his fledgling country through the Revolutionary War, the formation of its Constitution and the first eight years of its presidency. He was truly, as eulogized in Congress, "first in war, first in peace, and first in the hearts of his countrymen."

George Washington remains in the collective memory of America above all others through the many cities and counties which bear his name, including the State of Washington in the far west, and in the east, the City of Washington in the District of Columbia, the nation's capital. There, the **Washington Monument** soars above the city. In the Capitol Rotunda in Richmond stands the life like **Houdon Statue of Washington** and above the City of Alexandria rises the **National Masonic Memorial** and in Lexington is **Washington and Lee University.**

Last will and testament

George Washington's last will and testament of twenty-nine pages was probated in Fairfax County, Virginia. At that time, the courthouse was in Alexandria. The will was restored between 1909 and 1910 by William Burwick. He used a wheat flour and water paste to place a silk cover on each page to stabilize it from cracks and disintegration. For many years it was displayed at the old Fairfax Courthouse in a window and the exposure to light furthered its deterioration. In 1992, it was moved to the new Judicial Center and placed in a display case but had to be removed each night and placed in a vault. The will paper was either British or Dutch of a very high quality but George Washington had written on both sides. The ink used was also destructive and contributed to the deterioration of the paper. The document finally became too fragile and unstable and could not be displayed. In 2001, the will was restored again by Christine Smith. She placed the pages in an enzyme liquid which ate the flour paste and allowed her to lift the silk off the page. Once the silk was removed, Smith began the process to restore the paper. All fifteen sheets of the will were so carefully mended the repairs are not visible.

At the present time the will is kept permanently in a vault at the Office of the Clerk of the Circuit Court for Fairfax County, but a page at a time is loaned to Mount Vernon for display there. The entire will cannot be displayed until a temperature and humidity controlled environment can be provided.

Washington and Lee University

One of the oldest universities in the United States, Washington and Lee was started in 1749 as Augusta Academy. When it was relocated near Lexington, Virginia, in 1776, it was known as Liberty Hall Academy. George Washington bequeathed in his will to its "use and benefit" 100 shares of stock in James River Company. In appreciation, the school changed the name to Washington Academy in 1796. After a fire in 1803, the school was moved into Lexington and the name was changed in 1813 to Washington College. After the Civil War, Robert E. Lee served as its president until his death in 1870. It was Lee's father, Henry "Lighthorse Harry" Lee, a revolutionary war hero, who eulogized Washington as "first in war, first in peace, first in the hearts of his countrymen." It became Washington & Lee University in 1870 and Washington's gift remains a part of the University's endowment.

The magnificent statue of George Washington sculpted from carrara marble by Jean Antoine Houdon stands lifelike in the Rotunda of the Virginia Capitol surrounded by the busts of the other seven Virginia presidents, and the Marquis de Lafayette

Houdon statue of Washington

The marble statue of George Washington in the Rotunda of the Virginia Capitol in Richmond was the work of Jean Antoine Houdon. The project was commissioned by the General Assembly in 1784. The French artist, well known in Europe, was selected by Thomas Jefferson who was then Minister to France. Houdon journeyed to America just for the purpose of making a cast of Washington's face and to take the necessary measurements of his frame. The statue of carrara marble stunned the onlookers when it was unveiled, prompting even Washington's closest associates to claim it was his exact likeness. Imposing in its dignity, it captures the majesty and strength of the first president. It was first unveiled at the Louvre in Paris and after arriving in Virginia was placed in the Rotunda of the Virginia Capitol on May 14, 1796, where it has remained on continuous display. Houdon's signature and the date 1788 are on the statue (although it was not completed until 1791). On the five foot pedestal is an inscription of a resolution by the Virginia General Assembly, written by James Madison:

> The General Assembly of the Commonwealth
> of Virginia have caused this statue to be erected,
> as a monument of the affection and gratitude to
> George Washington:
> who uniting to the endowments of the Hero
> the virtues of the Patriot, and exerting both
> in establishing the Liberties of his Country
> has rendered his name dear to his Fellow Citizen,
> and given the work an immortal example
> of true Glory.

Visitors: The Capitol is open Monday to Saturday from 8:00 a.m. to 5:00 p.m., and Sunday from 1:00 p.m. to 5:00 p.m. There is a gift shop and a small café. Guided tours are available daily.

Directions: Capitol Square is in Richmond, Virginia, at 9th and Grace Streets.

Contact: Virginia State Capitol, 9th and Grace Streets, Richmond, Virginia 23219; (804) 698-1788; http://www.virginiacapitol.gov/; see also http://www.virginiamemory.com/online_classroom/shaping_the_constitution/doc/washington

The Washington Monument

George Washington resisted the idea of a memorial during his life because of the expense. After his death, one plan was to honor Washington with an equestrian statue. Another was to remove the remains of George and Martha from Mount Vernon and bury them beneath the floor of the Capitol Rotunda. Finally in 1833, a group of citizens formed the Washington National Monument Society and elected Chief Justice John Marshall as its first president. After Marshall's death, James Madison was elected president and in 1839 the Society's constitution provided that each President of the United States would be the honorary president. A fund raising campaign of one dollar from each person raised enough to select an architect, Robert Mills. He designed a obelisk surrounded by a circular colonnaded pantheon but the committee selected only the obelisk. A slight mound near the Potomac River was selected for Washington's monument to give it a greater sense of height. On July 4, 1848, the cornerstone was laid with the same trowel Washington had used to set the cornerstone of the Capitol in 1793. Only six years later, when the obelisk had reached a height of 152 feet, contributions dried up. Its unfinished remains looked down as the nation broke apart in civil war. Work was not resumed until 1880 when the Society gave the monument to the government. A clear line can be seen which marks the start of the new marble as it climbed to 555 feet 5 and 1/8 inches. The interior is open with an elevator and 898 steps. Memorial stones from cities, states, and countries, line the inner walls. On October 9, 1888, it was officially opened to the public. It is managed by the National Park Service.

Visitors: Open daily except July 4 and December 25; from 9:00 a.m. to 5:00 p.m., but 10:00 p.m. from Memorial Day to Labor Day. Free tickets are available on the day of the visit at the kiosk on the Washington Monument grounds at 15th Street and Madison Drive, first come, first served, from 8:30 a.m. Tickets may be reserved by telephone or website.

Directions: The monument is easily seen entering Washington, D.C. by either the 14th Street Bridge, or from the Lincoln Memorial Bridge or the Theodore Roosevelt Bridge onto Constitution Avenue. Metro stop: Smithsonian and Federal Triangle on the Blue Line.

Contact: The National Park Service, 1849 C Street, N.W., Washington, D.C. 20240; (202) 426-6841; www.nps.gov/wamo/planyourvisit/hours.htm

Washington Monument

The great obelisk rises high above the city that bears his name, the enduring symbol of America's patriarch.

A symbolic lighthouse, the George Washington Masonic National Memorial overlooks the port of Alexandria

54

George Washington Masonic National Memorial

On a majestic plateau in Alexandria, Virginia, the seven story George Washington Masonic National Memorial rises above the city. On Washington's birthday in 1910, the George Washington National Memorial Association was formed. Construction began in 1923 and the Memorial was dedicated on May 12, 1932. It is designed to create the effect of a "lighthouse" and took over ten years to build. The cost of construction was raised entirely from private donations from members of the Masonic community throughout the United States. The Replica Lodge Room and the Memorial Museum contain personal effects and Masonic items owned by Washington. This includes his bed chamber clock, stopped at 10:20 p.m., the time of his death. There are Twelve Dioramas which reflect events in Washington's life, and in the Memorial Hall is an imposing 17 foot high statue of Washington. There is also on display the key to the Bastille, presented to the lodge by the Marquis de Lafayette, when he visited Alexandria in 1825.

Washington joined the Fredericksburg Lodge when he was 20 and one year later became a Master Mason. In 1788, he became the Charter Master for the formation of an Alexandria Lodge, now the "Alexandria Washington Lodge." At his inauguration in New York, he used the bible from the St. John's Masonic Lodge, beginning the presidential tradition of taking the constitutional oath of office on a bible.

Visitors: Open daily from 9:00 a.m. to 5:00 p.m. for self guided tours for the first floor and mezzanine. Guided tours are daily at 10:00 a.m., 11:30 a.m., 1:30 p.m., and 3:00 p.m. for the Museum and observation deck. Closed Thanksgiving Day, Christmas Day and New Year's Day. Group tours available for 10 or more visitors.

Directions: From Interstate 95, take the Duke Street exit to King Street and the Memorial will be easily seen. From Washington D.C., go south on Mt. Vernon Boulevard to Alexandria and turn right on King Street to the Memorial. Metro stop: King Street-Old Town on Blue and Yellow lines.

Contact: George Washington Masonic National Memorial, 101 Callahan Drive, Alexandria, Virginia 22301; (703) 683-2007; www.gwmemorial.org/index.php

THOMAS JEFFERSON

The Third President

Birthplace: Shadwell

Date of Birth: April 13, 1743

Term: March 9, 1801 – March 3, 1809

Vice President: Aaron Burr 1801-1805
  George Clinton 1805-1809

Date of Death: July 4, 1826

Burial Place: Monticello

His words captured the spirit of a new nation
and became a promise for the world.

Early Years

The first Thomas Jefferson moved to the Virginia frontier along the eastern slope of the Blue Ridge in the late seventeenth century. By the time his grandson Peter Jefferson married Jane Randolph, the family was well regarded but not prosperous. Their oldest son was Thomas Jefferson, born on April 13, 1743 in the home *Shadwell* located east of Charlottesville. About three years after Thomas' birth, Peter Jefferson moved the family to *Tuckahoe* on the banks of the James River, south of Richmond. Peter had been named executor of the will of his close friend William Randolph and agreed to stay at Tuckahoe until Randolph's son was old enough to take control of the plantation.

Peter Jefferson ventured out to survey much of the Virginia wilderness and his map of Virginia prepared with Joshua Fry was for many years the most reliable. He returned his family to Shadwell on the banks of the Rivanna River when Thomas was about nine years old. Five years later in 1757, Peter Jefferson died, leaving Shadwell and the lands surrounding it to his oldest son.

Thomas Jefferson entered William & Mary in 1760. He left after two years to study law under George Wythe. It was not until 1767 that he returned to Albemarle County to build his law practice.

Jefferson the Lawyer

Jefferson maintained his law office, library and legal records at Shadwell. When it burned in 1770, it destroyed

---

Tuckahoe Plantation

When Thomas Jefferson was about 2 years old, his father, Peter Jefferson, moved the family to Tuckahoe Plantation west of Richmond on the north bank of the James River. Peter Jefferson left his own home at Shadwell to move his family to Tuckahoe on the death of William Randolph, cousin of Jefferson's wife Jane. Randolph had requested in his will that his "dear and loving friend" Peter, remain there until William's son, Thomas Mann Randolph, was grown. It appears Peter Jefferson only stayed six or seven years, not the length requested in the will. It was the place where Jefferson began his schooling at the age of five. In the approach to the plantation is the original one room school house where Jefferson studied as a boy on which hangs a plaque, "In this building Thomas Jefferson went to school 1748-1752." Constructed between 1733 and 1740, it was sold by the Randolph's in 1830. It is today owned by Mr. and Mrs. Addison Thompson.

Visitors: This is a private home and appointments must be made for guided tours of the house. Self guided tours of the grounds and pleasure gardens daily from 9:00 a.m. to 5:00 p.m., except when closed for special events.

Directions: Tuckahoe Plantation can be reached from I-95 (exit 83) on Parham Road south, to intersection with River Road, then west 4.6 miles. Enter country lane through while pillars just west of the dead end of Blair Road (Route 649).

Contact: Tuckahoe Plantation, 12601 River Road, Richmond, Virginia 23238; (804) 379-9554; www.tuckahoeplantation.com/

Shadwell
Birthplace of Thomas Jefferson

In the rolling foothills of the Blue Ridge Mountains east of Charlottesville near the Rivanna River lies the property Peter Jefferson called Shadwell. On it, he built a modest house and two years later, his eldest son, Thomas Jefferson, was born there. When Peter Jefferson died in 1757, Shadwell passed to Thomas Jefferson, but his mother had a life estate and continued to live there until it burned to the ground in 1770, destroying Jefferson's law books and case papers. The property on which Shadwell was located is on U.S. Route 250, 2.9 miles east of Charlottesville. It is owned by the Thomas Jefferson Foundation (owner of Monticello) and is not open to the public. The highway marker at the site reads:

Thomas Jefferson – author of the Declation Of Independence, third President of the United States, and founder of the University Of Virginia – was born near this site on 13 April 1743. His father, Peter Jefferson (1708 – 1757), a surveyor, planner, and officeholder, began acquiring land in this frontier region in the mid-1730s and had purchased the Shadwell tract by 1741. Peter Jefferson built a house soon after, and the Shadwell plantation became a thriving agricultural estate. Thomas Jefferson spent much of his early life at Shadwell. After the house burned to the ground in 1770, he moved to Monticello, where he had begun constructing a house.

his books and many of his legal papers, but he continued his efforts to establish a law practice. Elected to the House of Burgesses in 1769, he took a visible position in the increasing tension with Great Britain over the taxes imposed by Parliament on the colonies.

Jefferson did not possess great skill at public speaking but he had a remarkable talent for the felicitous phrase. In 1774, he wrote *A Summary View of the Rights of British America* spreading his reputation beyond Virginia. He was drawn to the great cause of his time, and after he was elected to the Second Continental Congress in 1775, his career in the courts was over.

Marriage

Martha Wayles Skelton was the young widow of Bathurst Skelton. She was living at Forest, the home of her father John Wayles in Charles City County, when she met and married Thomas Jefferson in 1772. She had a small son but he died the summer before her marriage to Jefferson. While still a student at William & Mary, Jefferson had cleared the top of a hill on lands inherited from his father and built a small pavilion. On the first day of 1772, he took his new bride through deep snows to that small building, afterward called the honeymoon dependency. It was later incorporated into his home which he called *Monticello,* "little mountain" in Italian.

A year later, Martha's father died and she inherited his estate, more than doubling the young couple's "ease of circumstances." The inheritance included the property in Bedford County on which Jefferson would later build *Poplar Forest.* To consolidate his holdings, he sold most of his property outside Albemarle County but did acquire a tract which included *Natural Bridge.*

Jefferson's marriage would last ten years, a period he called "unchequred happiness." Over this time, they would have six children, but Martha's strength gradually faded. She died four months after the birth of her last child and was buried in the *family graveyard at Monticello.* Only two of *Jefferson's children* would survive to adulthood.

Jefferson could watch through a telescope from his home at Monticello the construction of the University of Virginia in Charlottesville.

The Story of Monticello

Thomas Jefferson began the construction of Monticello in 1770 and continued to redesign and change it over the next 40 years. It sits on a mountaintop near Charlottesville, Virginia, on land Jefferson inherited from his father. After Jefferson returned from France, he completely redesigned Monticello. He was greatly influenced by Andrea Palladio, the 16th century Italian architect, and by two building he saw in Paris. He watched the construction across the Seine of the Hotel de Salm while taking his daily walk through the Tuileries gardens. The construction of the wooden dome on the Halle au blé (a central market in Paris) had been completed shortly before Jefferson arrived in Paris. In designing the Monticello dome, Jefferson's architectural and construction techniques are impressive even today. Monticello was the place Jefferson longed to be during his years in public life. At the end of his presidency he returned to Monticello never to leave except to visit Poplar Forest. It was Jefferson's hope that after his death, his daughter Martha and her children would continue to make it their home, but Jefferson's debts made that impossible. After his death in 1826, everything was lost to a public auction, first his household furnishings, farm implements and 130 slaves, and finally Monticello. In 1836, the house was conveyed to Uriah Levy and it eventually passed to his nephew Thomas Jefferson Levy, a member of the House of Representatives. The historic importance of the house guided the ownership by the Levy's, and the survival of the house is due to their care and maintenance over the next hundred years. Although great pressure was brought on Levy in the early 1900s to convey Monticello to the government, it was not sold until 1923 to the non-profit Thomas Jefferson Memorial Foundation.

Visitors: Now operated by the successor Thomas Jefferson Foundation, Monticello is open daily for guided tours of the house. Gates are open at 8:30 a.m. and closed at 7:00 p.m. Closed Christmas Day. Visitors may take self guided tours of the grounds and Family Graveyard.

Directions: From I-64 take Exit 121 to Route 20, then left on Route 53.

Contact: The Thomas Jefferson Foundation, 931 Thomas Jefferson Pkwy (GPS) Charlottesville, Virginia 22902; (434) 984-9800; www.monticello.org

The Story of Poplar Forest

Poplar Forest in Bedford County, Virginia, was inherited by Jefferson's wife, Martha, upon the death of her father in 1773. During the Revolutionary War, then Governor Jefferson, took refuge at Poplar Forest to avoid capture by a British cavalry raid on Monticello. It was during this stay at Poplar Forest that Jefferson compiled the research material for *Notes on the State of Virginia*, a book that has continued to create controversy over his description of African slaves. The construction of the unique octagon residence, influenced by the Italian architect Andrea Palladio, was not begun until 1806. Jefferson also incorporated design techniques, floor to ceiling windows, alcove beds, a skylight and an indoor privy he discovered during his stay in France. Jefferson's ownership of a second house was not well known, so Poplar Forest became a refuge from the endless stream of visitors to Monticello. He conveyed the estate in 1823 to a grandson, Francis Eppes, who sold it two years after Jefferson's death. It remained in private hands until it was acquired in 1984 by the non-profit Corporation for Jefferson's Poplar Forest. It is being restored to Jefferson's original design and offers a fascinating look at architectural archeology and colonial building techniques.

Visitors: Poplar Forest is open to the public daily, March 15 to December 30, from 10:00 a.m. to 4:00 p.m.; weekends only from January 1 to March 14 from 10:00 a.m. to 3:00 p.m.; closed Thanksgiving Day, Christmas Eve and Christmas Day.

Directions: Poplar Forest is southwest of Lynchburg in Bedford County. It is not easy to find, but do not be discouraged. There are detailed directions on the Poplar forest website at http://www.poplarforest.org/visit/directions

Contact: Thomas Jefferson's Poplar Forest, P.O. Box 419, Forest, Virginia 24551-0419; 1542 Bateman Bridge Road (GPS) Forest, VA 24551-0419; (434) 525-1806; www.poplarforest.org

Declaration of Independence

Although the Second Continental Congress had sent George Washington to Boston, many of the delegates hoped King George would acknowledge their rights as Englishmen. They did not wish war, only the repeal of the Intolerable Acts of Parliament and the removal of British troops from American soil. When the king responded by declaring the

Jefferson's Children

Martha (Patsy) was only ten when she accompanied her father on the long, mournful horseback rides in the hills about Monticello as Jefferson, "occasionally bursting into tears," struggled with the loss of his wife. Shortly afterward, he accepted an appointment as minister plenipotentiary to France. He took Martha with him and later, when he learned of the death of his youngest daughter, Lucy, he sent for Mary, his other surviving child. After his return from France at the end of 1789, Patsy married Thomas Mann Randolph, Jr., and resided at Edgehill, near Monticello. She later moved with eight of her children to Monticello when Jefferson returned from his second term as President. She spent the rest of her years as the mistress of Monticello until the house was sold at auction in 1831. Mary (Polly or Maria) was born in 1778, and when Jefferson went to Paris, she was left for several years at Edgehill. She later returned there as the bride of her cousin John Wayles Eppes. She was to die in 1804, at the end of Jefferson's first term as president, from complications in childbirth. The sorrow of her mother's similar death returned to Jefferson, and with only Patsy now surviving, he lamented that the happiness of his final years hung on "the slender thread of a single life."

colonies in rebellion, it added momentum to the call for independence.

Richard Henry Lee, of Virginia, rose before the Continental Congress on June 7, 1776, to offer a resolution that these "colonies are, and of a right, ought to be free and independent states, that they are absolved from all allegiance to the British crown, and that all political connection between them and the state of Great Britain is, and ought to be, totally dissolved."

Before voting on the resolution, the Congress appointed a committee to prepare a declaration of independence. This "draft committee" was composed of Benjamin Franklin of Pennsylvania, John Adams of Massachusetts, Robert Livingston of New York, Roger Sherman of Connecticut and Thomas Jefferson of Virginia. Adams proposed Jefferson as the draftsman because a Virginian was needed to

Natural Bridge

Virginia's natural "rock bridge" was surveyed by George Washington for Lord Fairfax in 1750. High up on the wall of the cliff below the arch can be seen what is believed to be the "mark" of George Washington, made when he surveyed the Bridge. Viewed on one of his travels, Thomas Jefferson called it "undoubtedly one of the sublimest curiosities in nature." Emotionally affected by its grandeur, he purchased the "rock bridge" and 157 acres from King George III in 1774. So many came to see this wonder, Jefferson constructed a small cabin to house visitors. Called the "bridge of God" by the Monocan Indians, the great limestone arch is 90 feet long, 150 feet wide at one end and 50 wide at the other and over 200 feet above Cedar Creek. Jefferson's estate was forced to sell Natural Bridge after his death. It is now located within Jefferson National Forest, near Lexington, Virginia in the upper Shenandoah Valley.

Visitors: One of the best sites in Virginia for the entire family, with a large gift shop and a Toy Museum in the Welcome Center. *Drama of Creation*, a narrated sound and light show, is presented nightly below the great arch. The Cedar Creek Nature Trail, from the Natural Bridge to Lace Waterfalls, with the Saltpeter Cave, the Monocan Indian Living History Village, and the mysterious "Lost River." Near the Welcome Center are the Wax Museum and Factory, with historical figures in narrated scenes. Caverns are the deepest commercial caverns on the east coast. Be sure to check the webpage as the hours of these attractions change during the year.

Directions: Natural Bridge is located at the intersection of U.S. Route 11 and Virginia Route 130, just south of Lexington. From I-81 take exits 180 or 175.

Contacts: Natural Bridge of Virginia, 15 Appledore Lane, Natural Bridge, VA 24578; (800) 533-1410 or (540) 291-2121; www.naturalbridgeva.com

show support from the southern colonies. Jefferson's skill as a writer and his revolutionary views were known in the colonies from his earlier paper, *A Summary View of the Rights of British America.*

After the Committee decided on the general points to be made, Jefferson prepared the declaration. What words

The Graveyard at Monticello

Jefferson left Monticello in trust to his daughter Martha (Patsy) to provide a lasting home for his family and his slaves, but his executors were forced to sell Monticello to pay his debts. Only a small graveyard was kept by the family. This had been started in 1773 with the burial of Dabney Carr, Jefferson's closest friend since boyhood, and the husband of his sister Martha. Jefferson is buried there beside his wife. In 1923, when the Thomas Jefferson Memorial Foundation purchased the house and property, an extension to the graveyard was added for "Jefferson's descendants." The stone obelisk that marks his grave is not the original monument which was replaced in the 1880's. The original obelisk was given by Martha Jefferson's family to the University of Missouri. The replacement was constructed according to Jefferson's design and reflects the inscription written by him. "As testimonials I have lived, I wish most to be remembered."

HERE WAS BURIED

THOMAS JEFFERSON

AUTHOR OF THE

DECLARATION

OF

AMERICAN INDEPENDENCE

OF THE

STATUTE OF VIRGINIA

FOR

RELIGIOUS FREEDOM

AND FATHER OF THE

UNIVERSITY OF VIRGINIA

Visitors: The graveyard is maintained by the Monticello Association. The public is invited to view the graveyard, but it is enclosed by a fence, so visitors cannot approach the grave markers.

Directions: The graveyard is located behind the house at Monticello.

Contact: The Monticello Association, http://www.monticello-assoc.org/history

were then contributed by others is not clearly known. To the revolutionaries gathered in Philadelphia these ideas on the *rights of man* were not original, but drew on the evolution of rights in England and the concepts of the European Enlightenment. Even the recently passed Virginia Declaration of Rights can be seen in its words.

Jefferson freely admitted it was not his object to create new principles. He had intended the Declaration to be an "expression of the American mind." So, indeed it became, and a promise to the world, that "all men are created equal, that they are endowed by their creator with certain unalienable rights, that among these are life, liberty and the pursuit of happiness."

The Rights of Man

At the conclusion of the French and Indian War in 1763, the colonists considered themselves loyal subjects of the king. It must be remembered that the thirteen colonies were English, tied by tradition, law and commerce to England. It was western thought and history that formed the foundation of social customs and political philosophy of all classes of citizens, including wealthy plantation owners such as George Washington and Thomas Jefferson. There was a profound shift in political and social thought throughout Europe in the 17th and 18th centuries. This attack on old dogmatism, both scientific and political, came to be known as the Enlightenment or the Age of Reason. The orderly universe of Isaac Newton, the natural laws of Frances Bacon, the empiricism of John Locke, the rule of law of Algernon Sidney, and the religious toleration of Voltaire were the vanguard of an intellectual movement which captured the imagination of British America. Many of the early charters of the American colonies were constitutions of a sort with various rights and obligations for both social and civil life. Gradually, the belief that rights were bestowed by the earth's creator came to be the accepted political thought in the colonies. Rights were natural to all men and documents did not create rights, but were the mere statement of those rights. Individual human dignity was not a grant by the government, but rather was inherent in the people.

The *signers of the Declaration of Independence* would have been satisfied to continue as British subjects if the King and Parliament had acknowledged their rights and satisfied their grievances. It had been the hope of many that the time would not come for British America to dissolve "the political bands" which connected them with England. They were caught in the momentum of their destiny, unleashed by their concept of liberty, which would carry them to a new form of government, not yet clear.

Religious Freedom

Thomas Jefferson was taught by Anglican clergy through his youth and during his years at William and Mary. The Anglican church, or Church of England, established by Henry VIII, was the official church of Virginia until the Revolution. Public officials swore to uphold the thirty-nine articles of Anglican faith. State and religion were intertwined.

Signers of the Declaration of Independence

The 56 signers of the Declaration of Independence were well known in their local communities, but at that time there were few that had a national reputation. Eight had not been born in America. There was one Roman Catholic and several Deists and the rest were Protestant. Six would later sign the Constitution. About one-third served as militia officers and four were taken prisoner by the British. Nearly one-third lost or had their homes damaged in the war. Most became poorer over the long years of conflict. All risked death for treason by signing, and affirmed in the closing line of the Declaration that "we mutually pledge to each other our lives, our fortunes, and our sacred honor." The Signers of the Declaration of Independence Memorial is set in a semi-circle and for each signer there is a stone block with his name, home town, occupation and a facsimile of his signature. The Memorial was a gift from the American Revolution Bicentennial Commission in 1976.

Visitors: The Signers Memorial can be visited at any time.

Directions: The Memorial is located on an island in Constitution Gardens Lake on the National Mall at Constitution Avenue opposite 19th Street, Washington, D.C. It is about midway between the Washington Monument and the Lincoln Memorial. Metro stop: Federal Triangle on the Blue Line.

Jefferson came to believe that it was not a function of government to enforce church law. He believed that religion was personal, not dictated by clerical authority. He wrote in the Declaration of Independence that "life, liberty and the pursuit of happiness," came directly to man from the "creator."

In 1776, Jefferson offered a new Virginia Constitution with a statement of full religious freedom. Later, in 1779, as Governor, he proposed a religious freedom statute as part of the revisals, "that Almighty God hath created the mind free," and that the "religious opinions and beliefs" of all men should be free from any control by the state. Strong opposition doomed that Jefferson effort.

Then, in 1784, a powerful coalition, which included John Marshall, Patrick Henry, and Edmund Randolph, submitted a bill to make Christianity the official religion of Virginia. All the churches would be supported by tax revenues. Jefferson was serving as Minister to France and was not there to oppose them. To the cause then stepped a young assemblyman who had supported Jefferson when the first bill was proposed in 1779. James Madison would prove equal to the task. First, he had Henry's bill bottled up. Then, Madison moved to enact Jefferson's Bill to Establish Religious Freedom. It was passed into law in January 1786. It is memorialized by the *Jefferson Religious Freedom Monument.* Madison wrote Jefferson that "the ambitious hope of making laws for the human mind" was forever banned in Virginia.

Minister to France

In the final months of the Revolutionary War, Jefferson's wife died. Distraught, he wanted to leave Monticello, and agreed to go to France as a commissioner to negotiate treaties. He would later become Minister to France, following in the footsteps of Benjamin Franklin. While in France, Jefferson received a request from directors appointed to construct a new *State Capitol at Richmond.* Jefferson decided to use a model of cubic architecture, the Maison Carrée, a Roman temple in Nîmes, France.

RELIGIOUS LIBERTY

FROM A MEETING IN FREDERICKSBURG,
JANUARY 13-17, 1777,
OF A COMMITTEE OF REVISORS
APPOINTED BY THE GENERAL ASSEMBLY
OF VIRGINIA, COMPOSED OF THOMAS
JEFFERSON, GEORGE MASON, EDMUND
PENDLETON, GEORGE WYTHE AND THOMAS
LUDWELL LEE TO "SETTLE THE PLAN OF
OPERATION AND TO DISTRIBUTE THE
WORK"- EVOLVED

THE STATUTE OF RELIGIOUS FREEDOM
AUTHORED BY
THOMAS JEFFERSON.

IN THIS DOCUMENT
THE UNITED STATES OF AMERICA
MADE PROBABLY ITS GREATEST
CONTRIBUTION TO
GOVERNMENT RECOGNITION OF
RELIGIOUS FREEDOM.

Jefferson Religious Freedom Monument

Jefferson's Bill to Establish Religious Freedom was enacted by the Virginia General Assembly on January 16, 1786. It has remained a statute in the Virginia Code since that time as the Act for Religious Freedom. It provides that, "Almighty God hath created the mind free...That no man shall be compelled to frequent or support any religious worship, place or ministry whatsoever, nor shall be enforced, restrained, molested or burthened, in his body or goods, nor shall otherwise suffer on account of his religious opinions or belief; but that all men shall be free to profess, and by argument to maintain, their opinions in matters of religion, and that the same shall in no wise diminish, enlarge or affect their civil capacities." It ends with the admonition that "we well know that this Assembly...have no power to restrain the acts of succeeding assemblies... yet we are free to declare, and do declare the rights hereby asserted are of the natural rights of mankind; and that if any act shall be hereafter passed to repeal the present, or narrow its operation, such act will be an infringement of natural right." The Thomas Jefferson Religious Freedom Monument, is located in Fredericksburg, Virginia at the intersection of Washington Avenue and Pitt Street. The Knights of Columbus conduct Religious Freedom Day each year in January in Fredericksburg to commemorate the contribution of the revisors.

Toward the end of Jefferson's stay in France, he was again at the center of a revolution. The French National Assembly passed the Declaration of the Rights of Man and Citizen in 1789. Although he was in touch with the Marquis de Lafayette and other leaders of the revolution, the extent of Jefferson's contribution to this document is not known. In the Rights of Man are echoes of the Declaration of Independence that "mankind is born free and equal," and that man has natural rights of "liberty, property, security and resistance to oppression."

Secretary of State

Jefferson had been away five and one-half years. He had missed the Constitutional Convention, although Madison had written him of the details. He had supported the addition of a Bill of Rights to preserve basic freedoms. When he returned to America at the end of 1789, waiting for him was a request by George Washington to become the nation's first Secretary of State. He joined the heads of other departments of the government in what came to be known as the president's cabinet.

It was soon divided, as was the country, over the war between France and England. The anti-Federalists, or Republicans, remembered that France had joined in a great alliance with the thirteen colonies that proved decisive in the revolution for American independence. They sought closer ties to France while the Federalists continued to feel a kinship with Great Britain. Jefferson was in constant conflict with the Federalist leader Alexander Hamilton over the direction of the new government. Hamilton advocated strong central control, particularly in the areas of taxation and finance. Jefferson felt that Hamilton wanted a country too much like the monarchy the colonists had fought to overthrow. Less than a year into Washington's second term, Jefferson resigned and returned to Monticello.

He returned to farming, developed a crop rotation system, started a nailery, and designed a new plow. However, the political world tugged him back and a reference in one of his letters ends his long friendship with Washington.

State Capitol at Richmond

Virginia moved its capital from Williamsburg to Richmond in 1780 and the committee responsible for construction of the new State Capitol wrote Jefferson, then Minister to France, for suggestions. Jefferson sent plans drawn by the French architect Charles-Louis Clerisseau based on the magnificent Roman temple at Nîmes, the Maison Carrée. Jefferson later described it as the "most beautiful and precious morsel of architecture left us by antiquity." A year later, Jefferson sent a plaster model of the Maison Carrée prepared by Jean-Pierre Fouquet. The model, remarkable in detail, was restored by Colonial Williamsburg Foundation and is now on display in the Capitol. In changing the Capitol to Jefferson's design, it was adapted to fit foundations already started and the great steps were eliminated to provide space for windows at the lower level. It was not until the early 1900's that the steps were added, restoring the impressive portico to Jefferson's concept. At the same time, the assembly halls were added on either side of the original structure and all the buildings were painted white. Although not completed until 1798, the Capitol was first occupied in October, 1788. Jefferson's decision to use the "cubic architecture" of the Maison Carrée introduced the classical form for public buildings to the United States. It remains in use today, the nation's second oldest Capitol. In the Rotunda of the State Capitol is the incomparable marble life-sized Houdon statue of Washington. In 1930, the General Assembly commissioned busts of the seven other Virginia presidents, and the Marquis de La Fayette. These surround Washington, displayed in niches in the Rotunda wall. On the grounds of the Capitol is the equestrian statue of Washington, designed by Thomas Crawford, unveiled in 1858 as a monument to Virginia's role in the Revolution. When the cornerstone was laid in 1850, it was attended by President Zachary Taylor and former President John Tyler. Surrounding the base of the monument are bronze statues of other Virginia figures in the Revolution, Andrew Lewis, Thomas Jefferson, Patrick Henry, Thomas Nelson, George Mason and John Marshall.

Visitors: The Capitol is open daily Monday to Saturday from 8:00 a.m. to 5:00 p.m. and on Sundays from 1:00 p.m. to 5:00 p.m. Guided tours are available daily.

Directions: Capitol Square is in Richmond, Virginia, at 9th and Bank Streets.

Contact: Virginia State Capitol, 1000 Bank Street, Richmond, Virginia 23219; (804) 698-1788; http://www.virginiacapitol.gov/

The Virginia state Capitol in Richmond modeled by Thomas Jefferson on the Maison Carrée in Nîmes, France

Alien and Sedition Laws

John Adams had served patiently for eight years as Washington's vice-president. He was the natural choice of the Federalists in 1796. Although Adams was elected, the vote was close and Jefferson, with the second highest total, became vice-president.

In order to suppress the supporters of France, Federalists in Congress passed the Alien and Sedition Acts. These four statutes gave President Adams the power to deport or jail aliens "dangerous" to the United States. The most controversial was the Sedition Act, which made it a crime to write or publish "false, scandalous, or malicious" allegations against the President, Congress or the government. To combat French subversion, the President was authorized to deport any alien "dangerous to the peace and safety" of the United States.

Jefferson believed the Sedition Act violated the guarantees of freedom of speech and press in the First Amendment. His resolutions against the acts were adopted by the Kentucky legislature and James Madison wrote similar ones for Virginia. This episode marked a major shift in public support to the emerging Jeffersonian republicans.

Revolution of 1800

Washington had united the country by the force of his personality. Upon his death, concerns about central power and taxation began to unite farmers, artisans and small businessmen. They had fought the Revolution expecting to have a voice in the new government. Many became "democratic republicans" and supporters of Jefferson.

The election of 1800 was the first election to be decided by the House of Representatives when Jefferson tied with Aaron Burr in the Electoral College. John Adams received less votes than either Burr or Jefferson and it has been a matter of historical dispute whether Jefferson's vote in the Electoral College was inflated by the *three fifths clause* in the Constitution. Jefferson felt his election was the final act in the revolution began twenty five years before. He would move to implement his view that government was not the sole province of the well-born but belonged to all the people.

In retaliation, a "northern conspiracy," led by New York, planned to create a group of states which would with-

---

Three-fifths Clause

When the Articles of Confederation were adopted in 1781, it authorized the Continental Congress to tax the states in order to fund the Revolutionary War. Under Article VIII, states would contribute in proportion to the "value of all land within each state." This formula was impossible to manage, so an amendment was proposed in 1783 to base taxation on the number of inhabitants. Because the slave system was not as efficient as free labor in the north, it was agreed to count slaves as 3/5th of a person. Two states rejected the new formula, so it did not become an amendment to the Articles. However, when the Constitution was adopted in 1788, the 3/5th formula was included as Article I Section 2 Clause 3 for both direct taxation of the states and for determining the number of representatives in the lower house of the new Congress. This compromise proved a benefit to the slave states as population became more important in determining the number of representatives than it did as a factor in tax assessment. Counting the slaves in the population increased the number of representatives allocated to a state in the House of Representatives, which increased the number of the electors in the electoral college.

draw from the Union and form a confederacy. One of the leaders was Aaron Burr, then Jefferson's vice-president, who attempted to become governor of New York. One of the reasons he was defeated was the opposition of Alexander Hamilton. Burr's loss of the presidency by the vote in the House of Representatives was due in part to Hamilton.

Burr felt these were personal attacks and challenged Hamilton to a dual. It was fought in Weehawken, New Jersey and Burr killed Hamilton. Burr, still vice-president, was indicted for murder in New York and New Jersey, but never tried.

Jefferson's inauguration day would begin a Virginia "dynasty" that would last for twenty-five years through the succeeding presidencies of James Madison and James Monroe.

Also, on that day as he took his oath of office, he looked into the face of a Chief Justice who would oppose his vision of limited government. *John Marshall* would lead the Supreme Court for 34 years and establish the judiciary as an equal branch with the presidency and the Congress in the development of the American federal system of government.

To the Shores of Tripoli

Even England, with its great naval power, found it easier to pay "tribute" than fight so its ships could pass the north coast of Africa unmolested by the Barbary pirates. The Revolutionary War brought an end to British protection of American shipping, so when an American ship was captured, the only way to secure its release was to pay tribute. Even George Washington reluctantly agreed to pay, but he also started the construction of naval warships.

After Jefferson became president, the pasha of Tripoli cut down the United States flag - a ceremonial declaration of war. He intended to frighten the young nation but the American reaction was, "Millions for defense; not one cent for tribute."

Jefferson understood that only Congress could issue a declaration of war. Undeterred, he responded to the

John Marshall

John Marshall was born in Fauquier County, Virginia, near Virginia Route 28. A Virginia highway sign .8 miles east of Midland notes the spot as "About one half mile southeast, just across the railroad, a stone marks the site of the birthplace, September 24, 1755." He was appointed Chief Justice of the Supreme Court in 1801 although he did not have much of a legal education - a six week course at William & Mary under the highly regarded George Wythe, also the teacher of Thomas Jefferson. Marshall was simple in dress, unaffected in manner, not someone who seemed ready to run the highest court in the land. He was the fourth Chief Justice in ten years and it may be no one else wanted the job. There was certainly no reason to believe his scholarship would establish the Supreme Court as the equal of the Congress or the presidency. A second cousin to Thomas Jefferson, the two represented opposite views on the power that should be exercised by the national government. During Marshall's 34 years on the Supreme Court, he tilted power away from the states and gave life to the balance of powers among the judicial, legislative and executive branches intended by the Constitution, and established the principle of judicial review. He died in Philadelphia July 6, 1835.

American outrage and sent four of the six newly built ships to the Mediterranean. He authorized retaliation if the U. S. ships were fired on. This decision by Jefferson laid the basis for future presidents to order American forces into battle even though Congress had not declared war.

The struggle with these pirates off the Barbary Coast lasted four years but no progress was made to release captured American sailors or to secure the right of ships to sail unmolested by the pirate bases. Finally, a dramatic 500 mile march across the Libyan desert by a makeshift Arab army held together by a detachment of Marines blocked the escape of the pirates by land from the city of Derna.

Bombarded by U. S. warships from the sea, the surrender of the city created pressure on Tripoli for a treaty that ended the war. The Marines became heroes, and stitched across their flag, "To the shores of Tripoli."

Purchase of the Louisiana Territory

France lost the French and Indian War, but devised a plan to keep the English from expanding their colonies west beyond the Mississippi River. France secretly ceded the Louisiana Territory to Spain in 1762. Later, Napoleon forced Spain to return it in 1800 by the Treaty of San Ildefonso.

Napoleon had plans for a renewed French empire based on control of the Mississippi. Once Napoleon landed his army in New Orleans, he would sweep up the Mississippi valley, block America's expansion to the Pacific and forever change the future of the young nation.

Saint-Dominque, the island called Hispaniola by Columbus and Santo Domingo by the Spanish, would be the base from which Napoleon would launch his invasion of New Orleans. Saint-Dominque had been the center of French trading in the western hemisphere but a slave revolt had erupted in 1791 and drove out the French. Napoleon was determined to reestablish French rule, but the resistance of the former slaves, yellow fever, and the war with England shattered this plan..

It was vital for American farmers in the west to have access to the port at New Orleans. Jefferson sent James Monroe to France to assist Robert Livingston in negotiations to purchase the port. To the surprise of the Americans, Napoleon was weary of the cost and loss of life to reconquer Saint-Dominque and he needed money for his war with England. He offered to sell the entire Louisiana Territory, 828,000 square miles; greater than the size of the original thirteen colonies.

The Constitution did not provide for the acquisition of foreign territory. Jefferson believed in limited governmental power and a "strict construction" of the Constitution. He drafted an amendment to the Constitution to authorize the Louisiana purchase. Fearful that Napoleon would back out during the delay in obtaining an amendment, Jefferson proceeded ahead and the potential constitutional issue was never seriously debated. A year later, Saint-Dominque was renamed Haiti.

Voyage of Discovery

Thomas Jefferson's inquiring mind contemplated the importance of the "western ocean." In 1803, he planned an expedition to cross the Louisiana Territory and map the route to the Western coast. This "corps of discovery" would gather data of plant life, animals and the soil and examine the possibilities of the fur trade in the inland waterways. Another purpose was to establish relations with the Indians. Jefferson felt at the time that so vast an expanse could hold both races.

Led by Meriweather Lewis and William Clark, this bold venture took twenty-seven months. They mapped the course of the Missouri and Columbia Rivers and finally dashed the old hope of a "northwest passage" to China through the great mountain ranges. They returned with plants, animal skins and even Indian chiefs, all to public acclaim. Some of the specimens may still be seen at Monticello.

Second Term

Despite his enormous popularity from the acquisition of the Louisiana Territory and his bold stand against the Barbary pirates, the federalist press kept Jefferson under a steady barrage of insult and innuendo. A charge which has survived over the years is that he had fathered children with his slave *Sally Hemings*. Jefferson ignored the attacks on his reputation and won an overwhelming approval for a second term.

Embargo

However, foreign affairs would soon turn sour and lead to an unhappy exit from the presidency. The European continent was again aflame with the Napoleonic wars and England began to seize American ships carrying French cargo. America was neutral but this was ignored by the British navy. American merchant ships were stopped on the high seas and sailors who could not prove American citizenship were removed. Jefferson viewed this impressment of American merchant seamen as kidnapping. To him, it was a

Sally Hemings

During his first term as President, Jefferson was faced with the public charge, first circulated in the Richmond Recorder newspaper by the journalist James Callender, that one of his slaves, Sally Hemings, was his mistress, and the mother of two of her children. Jefferson never replied publicly to this "Sally story," for he believed his character and reputation would refute the charge. Hemings had come to Monticello as one of the slaves inherited by Martha Jefferson on the death of her father, John Wayles. It has been assumed by many historians that Wayles was the father of Sally Hemings, but there is no proof of this. Several books, a miniseries, and a movie have claimed in recent years that Sally Hemings became pregnant by Jefferson in Paris. She had accompanied Jefferson's daughter Mary (Polly) to join Jefferson while he was Minister to France. Even to the present time, the Woodson family claimed that a Thomas Woodson was the Paris child of Thomas Jefferson and Sally Hemings. DNA tests in 1998 have shown this claim to be false. Sally Hemings' youngest son, Eston, was born in 1808 when Jefferson was 65 years old and President of the United States. DNA of Eston Hemings' descendants does link him to the Jefferson male line but does not establish that Thomas Jefferson was the father. Contemporary references to Sally Hemings are slight. Of all the Jefferson family who lived at Monticello, including the Hemings family, and those who would have been visitors and observers, none claimed during Jefferson's life that she ever attracted the slightest glance from him. Those who assert Jefferson's paternity rely heavily on a newspaper interview by Madison Hemings, given some forty years after he left Monticello. He recounts that his mother became pregnant with Jefferson's child in Paris, and refused to return to the United States until Jefferson promised that he would free all of her future children when they became twenty-one years of age. He does not relate the source of his information, and no other witness or document has ever supported his claim of a Paris child, or the so-called "treaty." A distinguished panel of thirteen scholars from universities throughout the United States studied this issue for more than a year. They issued *The Jefferson-Hemings Controversy: Report of the Scholars Commission,* with the "unanimous view that the allegation is by no means proven; and we find it regrettable that public confusion about the 1998 DNA testing and other evidence has misled many people into believing that the issue is closed."

violation of human rights and challenged the national sovereignty of the United States.

British arrogance pushed the issue to the edge of war when an American ship, the *Chesapeake*, was attacked off Cape Henry. Four sailors were taken off. There was an immediate uproar in America, but the British were unconcerned.

Napoleon closed the vise when he declared all ships trading with the British would be stopped. Caught between France and England, Jefferson and his Secretary of State, James Madison, decided to keep America out of harm's way until there was peace in Europe. American vessels, citizens and property were to be kept in American harbors. Jefferson convinced Congress to pass the Embargo Acts prohibiting foreign goods from entering American ports or American goods from leaving.

Unfortunately, the seaport towns of the east coast and the Great Lakes violently opposed the embargo because of the impact on their economies. Jefferson was soon faced with widespread insurrection and Congress was forced to lift the embargo.

Jefferson Returns to Monticello

When Jefferson left the presidency, the threat remained that the United States would be drawn into the war between France and England. Jefferson, with his unflagging optimism, still saw America as the world's "only monument to human rights." But, like a "prisoner released from his chains," he was relieved to turn over the reins of power to his successor James Madison. He went home to Monticello, never to see Washington again.

He was only days away from his sixty-sixth birthday. He could now pursue his love of gardening and his writing. His daughter, Martha, and eight of her children came to live at Monticello and Jefferson hoped to leave the great estate to her. He had tried to keep his expenses within his presidential salary but had to borrow money to clear his debts in Washington. Tobacco production at his farms had been seriously hurt by the embargo. Many of his slaves had grown old with him and they remained under his care. He had never been able to pay the debt which burdened the property inherited by his wife. Land values throughout Virginia slowly went down until his property was worth less than his debt.

The British burned the Capitol, which contained the *Library of Congress,* along with the White House and other public buildings in Washington in the War of 1812. Jefferson sold his library at Monticello, one of the finest private collections in America, to the Congress to replace the books destroyed by the fire.

In the years before he became President, Jefferson had designed the home of friends and relatives, the James Semple House in Williamsburg, *Belle Grove Plantation* and *The Residence at Woodbury Forest.* In his retirement, there was *Barboursville* and suggestions to James Monroe for *Oak Hill.* Jefferson had introduced the temple form for public buildings in the State Capitol at Richmond. He would continue this influence in his design for several *Virginia Courthouses.* Much of this would stretch into his final years when he undertook his most cherished endeavor.

Belle Grove Plantation

Belle Grove was completed in 1797 by Isaac Hite and his wife Nelly Conway Madison, sister of James Madison. Here, James and Dolley Madison spent their honeymoon. It is constructed of limestone from a quarry on the property in a design influenced by Thomas Jefferson. An extension was added in 1815 to complete the house as it looks today. From the mid 1800's it had a succession of owners until purchased by the National Trust for Historic Preservation and opened to the public in 1967.

Visitors: Tours daily Monday to Saturday from 10:00 a.m. to 3:00 p.m. and Sunday from 1:00 p.m. to 4:00 p.m.

Directions: From I-81, exit 302, west on Route 627, turn south on U.S. Route 11, then one mile south of Middletown, Virginia.

Contact: Belle Grove Plantation, 336 Belle Grove Road, P O Box 537, Middletown, Virginia 22645; (540) 869-2028; www.bellegrove.org

---

Library of Congress

Called "The Library of the United States" by Jefferson, it was established in 1800 in the new capital of Washington, to serve as the research arm of Congress. During the War of 1812, the entire collection was destroyed when the British burned the Capitol building where the books were housed. Beset by the bad debts which would follow him to his grave, Jefferson sold to the Congress his collection of books at Monticello, twice the size of the collection lost in the fire and considered the best private library in America. Almost 6,500 books, it became the nucleus of the new national library, but a second fire in 1851 destroyed much of Jefferson's contribution. In 1890, a cornerstone was laid for a new library structure and in 1897 it was opened to the public. It was renamed the Thomas Jefferson Building in 1980 and underwent a 15 year restoration before it was again opened to the public in 1997. Two other buildings have been erected, the James Madison Memorial Building and the John Adams Building.

Visitors: Hours are Monday through Saturday from 8:30 a.m. to 5:00 p.m. Closed Thanksgiving day, Christmas and New Years holidays. Pamphlets and phone apps available for a self-guided tour. Free guided tours are offered several times a day.

Directions: Behind the U. S. Capitol on Independence Avenue, the Library is easy to reach but parking can be difficult. Metro stop: Capitol South on the Blue and Orange lines.

Contact: Library of Congress, Thomas Jefferson Building, 10 First Street, SE, Washington, DC 20540; (202) 707-9779; www.loc.gov/index.html

The Residence at Woodberry Forest

This plantation house north of Orange, Virginia, was built by General William Madison, brother of the President, about 1793. Thomas Jefferson provided a floor plan for the seven room house and a Palladian portico. In 1870, Robert Walker purchased the home from the Madison family. He remodeled it in 1884 with a wing, open porches, dormers and an octagonal addition to the rear giving it the appearance it has today. Walker founded the Woodberry Forest School in 1884 and the house was renamed the Residence. It is the private residence of the Headmaster of Woodberry Forest School and is not open to the public.

The University of Virginia

As early as 1784, before he left for France, Jefferson devised a state-wide educational system with a university as the centerpiece. He tried unsuccessfully, as Washington had before him, to establish a national university in the new capital city of Washington. Then on October 6, 1817, Jefferson watched with two other presidents, James Madison and James Monroe, as the cornerstone was laid for Pavilion VII of the new Central College. It was in Charlottesville, about four miles from Monticello.

Shortly afterward, the Virginia General Assembly approved a new state university. Possible selections were the College of William and Mary in Williamsburg and Washing-

---

Virginia Courthouses

Even while his great project was going forward at the University of Virginia, Thomas Jefferson contributed to the design of several Virginia courthouses and continued to influence the use of the classical form for public buildings. The earliest was completed in 1820 at Fincastle in Botecourt County. This is in the upper Shenandoah Valley below Natural Bridge. Take exit 156 from I-81, onto State Route 640 then north on U. S. Route 220 to Fincastle. The courthouse was replaced in 1845, and there is some uncertainty whether Jefferson's plans were followed.

Several years later, Jefferson provided plans for a courthouse at Buckingham County. In 1869, fire destroyed the building. It was long believed that the building was replaced using Jefferson's original plans, although this assumption has been challenged. Originally called Maysville, the village is now Buckingham and is south of Charlottesville. It can be reached by taking State Route 20 to U. S. Route 60 and west to Buckingham, or on U. S. Route 20 from Amherst take U. S. Route 60 east.

During the time that Buckingham was constructed, the plans were also used to build the new courthouse for Charlotte County. Located at Marysville, it is the only remaining courthouse constructed before Jefferson's death. It is now identified on the map as Charlotte Court House and can be reached by U. S. Route 460 west from Richmond or east from Lynchburg. Exit at Pamplin City and go south about 20 miles on state Route 47.

---

ton College (later Washington and Lee University) in Lexington. Jefferson's offer of the Central College site was accepted and it became the University of Virginia. Calling it the "last of my mortal cares," Jefferson devoted his remaining years to his *academical village.*" He designed the architectural plan, supervised the builders, devised the curriculum and approved the instructors.

In 1816, America had only colleges and seminaries. Jefferson envisioned a range of study that would make this school a university. He was particularly anxious for a law school that would produce leaders to carry on his political vision.

Construction was not yet finished when the first class of students was enrolled in 1825. Jefferson was less than a year from death, and would not live to see the completion of his greatest achievement.

In speaking of his university, Jefferson left one of his most enduring phrases. "This institution will be based on the illimitable freedom of the human mind. For here we are not afraid to follow truth wherever it may lead, nor to tolerate any error so long as reason is left free to combat it."

The south elevation of Thomas Jefferson's Rotunda
facing the Lawn at the University of Virginia

Jefferson's "academical village"

Jefferson designed his "academical village" for a new Central College and along with James Madison and James Monroe, he set the cornerstone for the beginning of Pavilion VII. Construction began shortly before the Virginia General Assembly approved the site as the new University of Virginia. The design of the village featured a wide expanse of lawn, flanked by two parallel rows of buildings. At intervals in the rows Jefferson set Pavilions, two story structures which were occupied by the professors and where the students attended class and took their meals. Between the Pavilions were the student rooms which opened onto a colonnaded arcade that ran the length of the row and protected the students from the weather as they walked to the Pavilions for class and meals. This design permitted the row to be extended for additional Pavilions and student rooms as the population of the school increased. Behind these rows were the "ranges" of additional student rooms. It was suggested to Jefferson that he provide a dominant building as a focal point on the open north end of the two rows. There he placed his magnificent Rotunda, a domed structure modeled on the Pantheon in Rome. In 1976, the American Institute of Architects deemed his design of the University "the proudest achievement of American architecture in the past 200 years."

Visitors: Visitors to the "academical village" are welcome at any time. During the school year, tours of the Rotunda and the Lawn by student guides are offered every day at 10:00 a.m., 11:00 a.m., 2:00 p.m., 3:00 p.m. and 4:00 p.m. During the summer, tours are one-half hour for the Rotunda interior. Special tours are available. The Rotunda is open daily from 9:00 a.m. to 4:45 p.m., but check the website for the closings schedule.

Directions: From I-64, there are several exits to the University and the Rotunda. From U.S. Route 29, turn east on Business Route 250 to the Rotunda on the right. There is a parking deck at the intersection of 250/29.

Contact: Rotunda Administrator, University of Virginia, Charlottesville, Virginia 22904; (434) 924-7969; www.virginia.edu/rotunda

Barboursville

Barboursville was constructed between 1814 and 1821 by James Barbour, a Virginia governor, Senator, and Ambassador to Great Britain. Barbour asked his friend Thomas Jefferson to assist him with the design. The house was burned in 1884 and was never rebuilt but photographs reflect the similarity to Monticello. It contained an octagonal parlor and four Tuscan columns, a form Jefferson employed at Poplar Forest. Now known as the Barboursville Ruins, the walls still stand in mute memory of a lost age. Today, extensive vineyards cover the grounds and the winery is open to the public.

Visitors: Barboursville Vineyards and Historic Ruins are open Monday to Saturday from 10:00 a.m. to 5:00 p.m. and Sunday from 11:00 a.m. to 5:00 p.m. Closed Thanksgiving day, Christmas day, and New Year's day.

Directions: Barboursville can easily be included in a visit to Monticello or Montpelier. From U.S. Route 29 take U.S. Route 33 east to Virginia Route 20 then south to a left turn on Virginia Route 678 for 2 miles, then right on Route 777. From I-64 take exit 136 to U. S. Route 15 north. At Gordonsville, go west on Route 33 then left on Route 738, then south on Route 20 to a left on 678 for 2 miles, then right on Route 777.

Contact: Barboursville Vineyards and Historic Ruins, 17655 Winery Road, P. O. Box 136, Barboursville, Virginia 22923; (540) 832-3824; http://www.barboursvillewine.net/winery/estate-and-history

Only the walls of Barboursville remain after a fire destroyed the great home designed by Thomas Jefferson

Last Years

When the Virginia land values crashed in 1819, the prospect of erasing his debt became hopeless. Jefferson spent his last years knowing all would be lost. Yet, glancing backward, he felt that "the pleasures outweigh the pains of life." In his last letter to John Adams, with death in sight, his thoughts were of the "heroic age" when they had changed the world. Within days, he was dead.

In an astounding coincidence he died at Monticello on July 4, 1826, the fiftieth anniversary of his Declaration of Independence. More incredible was that John Adams, the only signer besides Jefferson to become President, died later the same day in Massachusetts. It would be more than a century later that a grateful nation, still guided by his words, erected the **Jefferson Memorial** in the nation's capital.

The most beautiful monument in the nation's capital, the Jefferson Memorial is an enduring symbol of a nation "dedicated to the proposition that all men are created equal."

Jefferson Memorial

Thomas Jefferson had placed a dome on his home at Monticello and on the Rotunda at the University of Virginia. John Russell Pope adopted this distinctive architectural feature for the Jefferson Memorial. It is supported by white marble columns around its circumference. One can look between the columns and see a 19 foot standing Jefferson, a bronze statue sculpted by Rudolph Evans. Inside, there are panels with the words of Jefferson that have come to define the promise of the country. Sitting beside the tidal basin and surrounded by cherry trees it has one of the capital's most dramatic settings. President Franklin Roosevelt requested Congress in 1934 to establish a memorial to Jefferson. It was dedicated on April 13, 1943, on the 200th anniversary of Jefferson's birth while a great war to determine the destiny of human freedom raged throughout the world. It is managed by the National Park Service.

Visitors: The Thomas Jefferson Memorial is located on the south bank of the Tidal Basin near downtown Washington, DC. It is open twenty-four hours a day. There is no charge to visit the Memorial. There is a book store and gift shop.

Directions: Getting to the Memorial by automobile can be a chore. It is on the south side of the Tidal Basin in West Potomac Park. The Memorial can be seen approaching Washington D. C. over the 14th Street Bridge. From the Washington Monument, go south on 15th Street (Raoul Wallenberg Drive) and follow the signs to Virginia. Stay to the right for the access road to the Jefferson Memorial. GPS Coordinates: 38.881387, -77.036508; Metro stop: Smithsonian on the Blue line. Public transportation at http://www.tourmobile.com/

Contact: Thomas Jefferson Memorial, 900 Ohio Drive, S.W., Washington, DC 20024-2000; (202) 426-6841; www.nps.gov/thje/index.htm

JAMES MADISON

The Fourth President

Birthplace: Belle Grove, Port Conway

Date of Birth: March 16, 1751

Term: March 4, 1809-March 3, 1817

Vice President:

> George Clinton 1809-1812
> Elbridge Gerry1813-1814

Date of Death: June 28, 1836

Burial Place: Montpelier

He guided the Great Convention of 1787 to the creation of the Constitution and the First Congress to the Bill of Rights, and the country to victory in the War of 1812.

Early Years

The son of James Madison Sr. and Eleanor Rose "Nellie" Conway, James Madison was born on March 16, 1751, on property now known as *Belle Grove,* in King George County, Virginia. When he was eleven years old, he began his formal education in Donald Robertson's school in King and Queen County, Virginia. After five years, he was tutored at home by Thomas Martin, a graduate of the College of New Jersey, which later became Princeton University. This may have influenced Madison who chose to attend college there rather than in Virginia. He received his degree in September, 1771 after two years of intense study. He remained in school another eight months due to his concern he was not strong enough to make the trip home.

When Madison returned to his father's home *Montpe-*

Thomas Jefferson would later call him the "country's greatest farmer," Madison did not feel when he returned from college that life held much in store for him. He worried whether his poor health would lead to an early death.

The Cause of Religious Freedom

In April, 1776, Orange County, where the *James Madison Museum* may be found, selected Madison as a delegate to the Second Virginia Convention in Williamsburg. This Convention adopted George Mason's Declaration of Rights on the eve of the Revolutionary War. Mason had proposed "the fullest toleration in the exercise of religion," but young Madison went further. His attitude on religious freedom was

The Story of Montpelier

An original plantation house was built on the property about 1732 by James Madison's grandfather. The property was called Mount Pleasant and the original house was in the vicinity of the present Madison family cemetery. Mount Pleasant was Madison's home until he was nine when his father built the central portion of Montpelier about 1760. It is not known precisely how the name Montpelier was given to the new house but the use of the name first appears in 1781 and was generally used by the family after that. The French word Montpellier, means "mount of the pilgrim," and was known for its wholesome climate, perhaps believed to also describe the area of the Madison house. When James Madison brought his new wife Dolley to Montpelier it was still occupied by his father but on his death in 1801 the property became Madison's. He enlarged it by adding the two wings and the portico. After Madison's death, Dolley moved to Washington, but the mismanagement of Montpelier by her son forced her to sell it in 1844. The property passed through a series of private hands but in 1983 the last owner, Marion duPont Scott, transferred the property to the National Trust for Historic Preservation. It has been open to the public since 1987, while restoration and archeology of the site continues. Except for the temple ice house all the out buildings associated with the original plantation have disappeared. The house was altered and greatly enlarged during the eighty-two years it was owned by the duPont family. After a twenty year study, it was decided to return the house to the appearance it had in Madison's time.

Visitors: Montpelier is open Tuesday through Sunday, November through March from 10:00 a.m. to 4:00 p.m., and April through October from 9:00 a.m. to 5:30 p.m. It is closed Thanksgiving, Christmas, and the first two weeks in January. See http://www.montpelier.org/visit/. Stop at the Visitor's Center to purchase tickets and visit the gift shop.

Directions: Watch for the Montpelier entrance four miles southwest of Orange, Virginia, on Route 20, or approximately 40 miles northeast if traveling from Charlottesville, at 11407 Constitution Highway, Montpelier Station, VA 22957

Contact: James Madison's Montpelier, P.O. Box 911, Orange, VA 22960; (540) 672-2728; www.montpelier.org

Montpelier, now restored to the changes made by James Madison, looking west across the most imposing front yard view in America. The vista that greeted Madison remains the same today.

The James Madison Museum

Located in the town of Orange, about 15 minutes from Montpelier, the James Madison Museum features exhibits on James and Dolley Madison. It has numerous personal items and furnishings, including Madison's favorite chair, a Campeche given to Madison by Thomas Jefferson. There is a small gift shop. The museum is owned and operated by the James Madison Memorial Foundation.

Visitors: It is open Tuesday to Saturday 10:00 a.m. to 4:00 p.m.

Directions: Orange is at the junction of Virginia Route 20 and U. S. Route 15. It can be reached from U. S. Route 29 by Virginia Routes 15 or 33, and from I-95 by Route 3 from Fredericksburg, then Route 20 to Orange, or from I-64 from Richmond, then north on Va Route 15

Contact: The James Madison Museum, 129 Caroline Street, Orange, Virginia 22960; (540) 672-1776; www.thejamesmadisonmuseum.org/

reflected in his amendment that "all men are equally entitled to the free exercise of religion, according to the dictates of conscience." Madison had freed man's religious belief from control by the state.

Some months later, Madison was back in Williamsburg as a member of the first House of Delegates. The Revolution had ended the status of the Anglican Church as the official state church. Still, there was strong support for an official church and to use taxes to fund salaries for the clergy. Madison helped to defeat this effort. At this point, Thomas Jefferson attempted to place in the new Virginia constitution a full guarantee of religious freedom, but this effort was rejected. After he became governor in 1779, Jefferson submitted the bill again. Madison tried to maneuver it through the General Assembly, but again it was unsuccessful.

After Jefferson left to become Minister to France in 1784, a powerful coalition in the General Assembly proposed to make Christianity the official religion of Virginia. Taxes would pay the salaries of the clergy of all Christian denominations. Madison led the defeat of this assessment. With momentum in his favor, he placed Jefferson's bill back before the General Assembly. This time it passed. Although he noted there were "some mutilations in the preamble," Jefferson included the authorship of the Bill to Establish Religious Freedom as one of his greatest achievements. Madison, the loyal friend and political ally, never intruded his great contribution on the credit due Jefferson.

The War Years

Madison was defeated in his re-election bid to the General Assembly in 1777. Later, he won a seat on the governor's council. He served first under Patrick Henry and then in 1779 under Thomas Jefferson. In 1780, Madison became the youngest member of the Continental Congress.

He never served in the military during the Revolutionary War but his political experience over these years would prepare him for the great task ahead.

In 1785, representatives from Virginia and Maryland met at Mount Vernon to negotiate an agreement to share the use of the Potomac River. It became clear that the issues of trade and navigation could not be settled unless all the states were present. James Madison urged a second meeting in Annapolis. Little was accomplished because delegates from only five states showed up. Three of the most important, New York, Pennsylvania and Virginia did attend. This presented an opportunity for Madison and Alexander Hamilton to urge another meeting in Philadelphia to address the lack of a central authority in the *Articles of Confederation*. Thus, the stage was set for what became the Constitutional Convention of 1787.

Constitutional Convention of 1787

The delegation elected to represent Virginia at the Convention, called at this time a "General Convention," or a "Federal Convention," was George Washington, George Mason, Edmund Randolph (who would become the country's first attorney general), and James Madison. Madison had devoted the spring and summer of 1786 to a study of the

---

Articles of Confederation

The Articles of Confederation, adopted in York, Pennsylvania, recognized the sovereignty of each of the thirteen states, although they were collectively called the "United States of America." The Articles were essentially a treaty between the former colonies to provide for the contribution of men and money for the war of independence against England. There were also provisions for treaties with foreign powers, printing money, managing Indian affairs and establishing post offices. All of this was to be coordinated by a committee made up of two representatives from each state. Regardless of its size each state had one vote. However, the Articles of Confederation failed to establish a national government. A major weakness was the lack of authority to enforce the collection of money from the states to pay the cost of the war. The thirteen original states were New Hampshire, Massachusetts, Connecticut, New York, Rhode Island, New Jersey, Pennsylvania, Delaware, Maryland, Virginia, North Carolina, South Carolina and Georgia.

---

strengths and weaknesses of confederations and republics. Much of his research was in books sent to him by Jefferson who was now in Paris as Minister to France.

Madison summarized his findings in a booklet, "Ancient and Modern Confederacies." He analyzed historical and current governmental structures to determine how a government must function to preserve the right of the people to control the succession of power.

When the convention opened, Edmund Randolph submitted the Virginia Plan prepared by Madison. It was now clear to all the delegates that they were embarked on a trip not planned. They had been sent by their states to amend the Articles of Confederation, but they were headed toward something new.

The only state that did not send representatives was Rhode Island, which later refused to ratify the Constitution. The Convention proceeded as planned through the hot summer of 1787, presided over by George Washington, elected President of the Convention by unanimous agreement of all the delegates.

As Madison wrote to Jefferson, the "objects of union" could not be reached by a confederation of states. It was necessary for the people to empower both the states and a national government. Madison wrote that in Europe, "charters of liberty are granted by power," but in America, these charters of power are "granted by liberty." When the new form sought a name because it was not like any before, Madison termed it a republic, because it derives "all of its powers directly or indirectly from the great body of the people."

The principle which Madison believed essential to guarantee freedom was the dilution of power. It was the conventional wisdom that democracy could not flourish in a large republic because the majority would always control the minority. Madison wrote that the solution was a "great variety" of citizens and beliefs so a majority could not be formed unless it sought "justice and the general good." He also recognized that a federal system spread power among the states and the central government. This would create checks and balances among the many departments of government and through many levels of elected and appointed officials.

Still, there was great fear among the delegates that the larger states, such as Virginia, would be able to dominate the new Congress.

A New Jersey Plan was presented on behalf of the "small states" to keep a one house legislature in which each state would have equal representation. Finally, a Connecticut "compromise" broke the deadlock by a proposal that Congress have two houses, one with representation determined by population, and a senate in which each state had an equal vote.

Gift of the People

Although the Articles of Confederation required an agreement of all thirteen states, the delegates to the Convention took it upon themselves to provide that only nine states were needed for ratification of the Constitution. Each state held a convention to decide that state's vote. By the time the nine required states had ratified the Constitution, the conventions of two states, New York and Virginia, had not yet met. There could not be a *United States of America* unless these two were included. Virginia was the largest state, and divided the colonies, north and south. Without New York, the New England colonies were divided. The enormous effort to produce the *Federalist Papers* was necessary to convince New York voters to ratify the Constitution.

George Mason and Patrick Henry opposed ratification. "Virginia's great dissenters" argued to the Virginia Convention that a fundamental bill of rights must be clearly stated in the Constitution. Mason had authored Virginia's Constitution and its Declaration of Rights. Henry had served as Virginia's first governor and was known for his fiery patriotism in urging revolution.

Madison believed that a special Bill of Rights was not needed because the government had only the powers specifically given to it as a "gift of the people." To overcome the opposition generated by Mason and Henry, Madison promised the Virginia delegates that he would propose a bill of rights in the new Congress to protect fundamental rights. On this condition, Virginia narrowly approved the Constitution 89-79.

The New York vote was also close, by the narrow margin of 30-27. The ratification was complete but it was far from certain that the new Constitution would survive. Three states besides Virginia—Massachusetts, New Hampshire and New York—had ratified the Constitution on the

---

The United States of America

The term United States of America was used in the Declaration of Independence, but in the war against England, the colonies considered themselves independent states bonded together by "friendship." The only central authority was the Second Continental Congress. When the Articles of Confederation were ratified in 1781, it declared that "each state retains its sovereignty, freedom and independence," although the term United States of America was again used. In the Paris Treaty (Peace Treaty of 1783), which ended the Revolutionary War, England gave formal recognition to the United States of America, but declared the former colonies "free sovereign and independent states." The Constitution ratified in 1788 used the term "We the people of the United States" in the preamble. For the next seventy-five years it was debated whether the individual states retained their sovereignty in the new nation or whether the peoples of the various states were bonded together as one. As early as 1800, when Jefferson was elected, Federalists in northern states threatened to secede. The issues of slavery and tariffs caused certain southern states to threaten secession which led to the Missouri Compromise in 1820 and the Compromise of 1850. This period even spawned a doctrine of nullification which held that an individual state had the right to ignore laws of the federal government. The issue would be finally resolved by a terrible loss of 600,000 lives and vast destruction of property across the southern states in the American Civil War, and the subsequent adoption of the 13th, 14th and 15th Amendments to the U. S. Constitution. The 13th Amendment, which abolished slavery, mirrored the words of the Northwest Ordinance, written by Thomas Jefferson.

condition that certain civil rights were to be more clearly stated. Two states— Rhode Island and North Carolina— rejected the Constitution.

Bill of Rights

In order for Madison to make good on his pledge, he first had to be elected to the new Congress. Senators were to be chosen by the Virginia General Assembly and Patrick Henry influenced the Assembly to select two opponents of the Constitution. Madison's last chance was a seat in the House of Representatives, which was decided by popular vote. Madison won in a difficult campaign against James Monroe, an opponent handpicked by Henry.

Thomas Jefferson also favored a bill of rights. He wrote from France that the Constitution was "good, but not perfect," and that he hoped that the states "annex to it a Bill of Rights..." Madison realized that the widespread demand for a bill of rights could result in a new Constitutional Convention. If that happened, the Constitution might be undone.

Federalist Papers

The Constitutional Convention adjourned on September 17, 1787 and sent the new Constitution to the state conventions for ratification. A series of 85 letters (or essays) appeared in the New York newspapers between October, 1787 and April, 1788. These letters explained the federal system outlined in the proposed Constitution. It was the idea of Alexander Hamilton to use the letters to gather popular support for ratification in New York. He enlisted John Jay, who would become the first Chief Justice of the Supreme Court, and James Madison, who would become the nation's fourth president, to contribute letters, all under the name Publius. The letters argued for a stronger union and described how the branches of the government would work and the relationship of the central powers to the sovereignty of the states. They were later published in two volumes called The Federalist, but now are often referred to as The Federalist Papers. A list made by Hamilton, found after his death, created a controversy over the authorship of certain letters. It is generally accepted that Hamilton authored 51 of the essays, Madison 29 and Jay 5.

Madison reviewed all of the amendments proposed at the state ratifying conventions. He guided the new Congress to adopt twelve amendments which went back to the states for ratification. Ten were approved and became the American Bill of Rights and Madison became known as the "father of the Constitution."

A More Perfect Union

The *Founding Fathers* had achieved, for their posterity, the most significant advancement in mankind's long struggle to form a just society. They had created an executive who served at the will of the people, and whose power to act was balanced by an elected legislature and an appointed judiciary. They made government subject to a written law of the land and guaranteed freedom and liberty to each citizen. They preserved the sovereignty of the states, but created a direct relationship of laws and services between the central government and the people.

The Constitution was not the work of government but of the people, and it could not be changed by government, but only by the people. This was the concept that would change the world.

Equality did not mean all the citizens had an equal station in life. Rather, it meant freedom from governmental control, freedom to practice a selected religion, freedom to speak and write what they pleased, and most of all, to own property free from government regulation. But these rights were mostly for white men. Not mentioned in the Constitution was *slavery*, although it is the subject of ten separate provisions. Native Americans were not citizens. Women were not given the right to vote. For some, the promise of equality lay in the future.

Philadelphia Years

Madison agreed with Jefferson that this would be a country of farmers, moving westward, building self-sufficient communities. This vision was different from that of Alexander Hamilton. He planned for the federal government to assume the debts of the Revolutionary War, to cre-

Founding Fathers

The term Founding Fathers is generally given to the 55 men who came to Philadelphia in the summer of 1787 and took part in what was later called the Constitutional Convention of 1787. Thirty-six had served in the Continental Congress and six had also signed the Declaration of Independence. Two would become president, George Washington and James Madison. The term is often used to include all of the signers of the Declaration of Independence and the Articles of Confederation. Two who signed the Declaration but did not attend the Constitutional Convention became president—John Adams, then Minister to England, who published a book, *A Defense of the Constitutions of Government of the United States of America*, and Thomas Jefferson, then Minister to France, whose promise of equality in the Declaration of Independence was a challenge to the Convention. The term has sometimes included those who contributed greatly to the founding of the nation. Although a member of the Constitutional Convention, the Virginian George Mason refused to sign the new Constitution because it did not have a Bill of Rights.

ate a national bank, and to tie the trade and commerce of the United States to England. Madison had worked closely with Alexander Hamilton to bring about the adoption of the Constitution and the federal system. He was now the voice in Congress against Hamilton's policies.

Madison was accepted as the leader of the emerging "republicans." He was also newly married, his bride the vivacious widow Dolley Payne Todd. She was born in North Carolina but lived a portion of her youth in *Scotchtown,* later the home of Patrick Henry. Her daring during the British invasion of the Capitol in the war of 1812 would make *Dolley* an American icon.

At the end of his first term, George Washington desired to return to private life. Madison prepared for him a final address to the American people. It was not given because the opinion was universal that Washington should seek a second term. Four years later, he did use Madison's suggestions in the now famous Farewell Address. He also sought the advice of Alexander Hamilton. It was time too, for Madison to return to the life of a farmer at Montpelier.

Scotchtown

Shortly after Dolley Payne was born in 1768, her father returned the family to Hanover County, Virginia. For a short time her parents rented Scotchtown, later purchased by Patrick Henry. Dolley's mother was Henry's first cousin and it is not clear if the family remained in the house after Henry's purchase in 1771. Dolley lived in this area until the family moved to Philadelphia in 1783. A portrait in one of the dining rooms commemorates Dolley's stay. Scotchtown was built in 1719 in a community settled by Scottish immigrants. Patrick Henry was Virginia's first governor when he owned Scotchtown, leaving there in 1778. The house was in deplorable condition when, largely through the efforts of Noreen Campbell, it was purchased in 1958 by the Association for the Preservation of Virginia Antiquities. After it was restored, Scotchtown was opened to the public in 1964.

Visitors: Guided tours March through December, Friday and Saturday from 10:00 a.m. to 5:00 p.m. and Sunday from 1:00 p.m. to 5:00 p.m. Please arrange group tours one week in advance. Small museum shop. Closed Easter, Mothers Day, July 4 and Christmas Day.

Directions: From I-95, U. S. Route 1, or U. S. Route 301, take State Route 54 approximately 10 miles west to State Route 671, left to State Route 605. Route marked by Scotchtown signs. From western Virginia take U. S. Route 33 to Route 54.

Contact: Scotchtown, 16120 Chiswell Lane, Beaverdam, VA 23015; (804) 227-3500; https://preservationvirginia.org/visit/historic-properties/patrick-henrys-scotchtown

Dolly or Dolley?

She was originally Dolley Payne, then Dolley Payne Todd and finally Dolley Payne Madison, but her signature was usually D. P. Madison. However, her early biographers spelled her name Dolly and there are sources that claim that her real name was Dorothea. Many products appropriated the name and at one point the Encyclopedia Britannica called her Dorothy. The dispute was finally settled in 1958 when the Smithsonian added Dolley Madison's 1809 inaugural gown to its first ladies collection. The Papers of James Madison at the University of Virginia determined that the owner of the gown was Dolley.

Slavery

One of the harsh realities of colonial life was slavery. The issue divided the northern and southern states at the Constitutional Convention. The Constitution could not have been adopted unless slavery and the slave trade were permitted to continue. The delegates to the Convention were aware of the stark contrast between the equality proclaimed in the Declaration of Independence and the presence in the new nation of vast numbers of Africans held in slavery. When the Constitution was ratified by the states in 1788, the words "slave" or "slavery" were not used, but the reality of the institution was addressed in ten separate provisions. Six states had abolished slavery before the Constitutional Convention and two followed shortly afterward. In Virginia, slaves could be freed by personal manumission. Efforts by those owners who wished to free their slaves were frustrated by laws which required freed slaves to leave the state within one year, and made the former owner responsible for them during that time. By 1798, all states except South Carolina denied the right to import slaves. In 1808, in one of his last acts as president, Thomas Jefferson signed the bill that abolished the slave trade and it was thought that slavery would eventually die out. However, the slave population continued to increase since laws in the slave states made a child born to a slave mother a slave. All of the Virginia presidents except Wilson were slave owners.

Secretary of State

Although a private citizen at Montpelier, Madison continued to oppose the federalism of President John Adams. He wrote the Virginia Resolutions against the Alien and Sedition Laws that the Federalists had enacted to suppress opposition to their policies. Madison was instrumental in the rise of anti-federalist feeling which swept Thomas Jefferson to victory in the election of 1800. James Madison returned to the nation's capital as Jefferson's Secretary of State.

When Napoleon made his astounding offer to sell the Louisiana Territory, Madison urged Jefferson to accept. Jefferson was concerned about whether the Constitution permitted a president to buy land from a foreign country. Madison argued it was the natural course for a nation to expand. Madison's view of government was broader than the limited government of the "old republicans." He saw an important role for the federal government in the lives of the people.

James Madison's greatest challenge as Secretary of State was to keep the young nation out of the war between England and France. George Washington had steered a neutral course. President Jefferson and Madison tried to do the same, but American neutrality was ignored by England. American trading ships were routinely stopped. Often American seaman were taken off and forced into the British navy.

Finally, Jefferson imposed an embargo to keep American ships safe in American ports. However, opposition to the embargo by states on the east coast was so intense it was finally lifted.

James Madison was selected by the Republicans to succeed Jefferson as president. In Virginia and North Carolina, a group of "old republicans" backed James Monroe. They felt the small, quiet Madison lacked the energy and forceful personality required of a president. Monroe permitted his name to be used but did not campaign and received no electoral votes. There was widespread opposition to Madison in New England because of the Jefferson trade embargo against England. In spite of the sectional differences in the country, Madison was a clear winner.

War of 1812

As England and France warred, America was caught between them. Its ships were attacked by both sides and the British navy continued to impress American seamen, violate U. S. territorial waters and blockade its ports. Finally, it became too much for the young country to bear. Spurred on by the "War Hawks" in Congress, from the west and south, the United States declared war on June 18, 1812, on the most powerful nation in the world.

Madison faced an array of problems. The country was divided on the war. Support came from the southern and rural states, but Federalists in a number of the northern states refused to send men or raise taxes. It was difficult for Madison to hold the nation together. Congress balked at providing funds. Anticipated revenues from the sale of public lands in the southwest did not come in because of the depressed economy.

Those Americans anxious for war against England wanted more than retaliation and to uphold the national honor. They wanted Canada. Ill prepared for war, America's early attempts to move into Canada failed. Then, Oliver Hazard Perry cleared the British navy from Lake Erie. William Henry Harrison routed the Redcoats and Indians in the Battle of the Thames. After the Battle of Sackets Harbor, the British abandoned Lake Ontario.

As 1813 ended, England still held the Canadian border. It had also defeated Napoleon, so Great Britain shifted men from the war with France to America. It launched new offensives in the north and reinforced the blockade of the Atlantic Coast. To the watching nations of the world, it seemed England would reclaim her colonies.

With the American armies pinned down in the north, the British navy sailed unmolested into the Chesapeake Bay and landed troops on the Maryland shore, at the mouth of the Patuxent River, some sixty miles south east of Washington. Panic set in as the Redcoats marched on the nation's capitol.

A small American force was brushed aside at Bladensburg, Maryland, so President Madison and the government fled into the Virginia countryside. Enemy soldiers entered the deserted city on August 24, 1814 and the ***burning of Washington*** began. The British troops burned the Capitol, the White House and most of the government buildings before returning to their ships the next night. A timely storm helped put out the flames and prevented more destruction.

The Dawn's Early Light

It was not so easy for the British in Baltimore. American regular troops and militia put up a stout defense. Fort McHenry withstood the naval bombardment and by "the dawn's early light" Francis Scott Key penned the words to the Star Spangled Banner. The British navy sailed away but it still had another plan. It would attack the United States from the south, at New Orleans.

Congress debated moving the capital to another city, but decided to rebuild Washington. *Octagon House* became the residence for President Madison while the White House was restored.

Burning of Washington

Unfazed by the approaching British army, Dolley Madison waited while servants struggled to detach the large portrait of George Washington by Gilbert Stuart from the wall. Finally, she ordered the frame broken so the canvas could be removed. Fearful of damage to the painting, it was cut from the frame with a pen knife. With the picture and other valuables from the White House, she sought refuge at Belle Vue in Georgetown (now known as Dumbarton House). It is believed Dolley then went to Belmont near Leesburg. Belmont was build by Ludwell Lee around 1800 and is today a part of the Belmont Country Club. It can be seen from U. S. Route 7, several miles east of Leesburg. James Madison stayed the night in Fairfax County at Salona which today is privately owned and not open to the public. Finding that his wife was safe, he crossed the Potomac and joined the army. He stayed in Brookville, Maryland, in a home now called the Madison House which has been restored and is privately owned. Madison may have sought out a Quaker family at the house because Dolley Madison had been a Quaker before her marriage. Records and valuable papers from the Department of State, including the Articles of Confederation, the Declaration of Independence, the Constitution, the correspondence of General Washington, and the secret journals of Congress were transported to Leesburg. There is some mystery where the government records were stored. It has been a long tradition that they were taken to Rokeby, outside Leesburg. A letter describing the place as a vacant house with a vault fits the description of Rokeby, then owned by the Sheriff of Loudoun County. Rokeby is privately owned and not open to the public.

Hartford Convention

Even while the country struggled for its existence, the Federalists held the Hartford Convention to discuss secession from the Union. With that threat as a weapon, the Federalists proposed a number of amendments to the Constitution. One would limit the president to one term and his successor to a different state. This would break the "Virginia Dynasty." Another would require a two-thirds vote of Congress for new states to join the union. This was designed to bar any more agricultural states.

After the war, the public found out about the Hartford Convention. There was widespread outrage when it was revealed the Federalists had secretly negotiated with the British. An overwhelming mandate given in the election of James Monroe was the death-knell of the Federalist party.

Victory at New Orleans

As 1814 drew to a close, the peace negotiators finally agreed to end the war. Unfortunately, this news did not reach the British expedition which sailed from Jamaica to attack the Americans at New Orleans. The news of peace was also unknown to the waiting American force under Andrew Jackson.

The Redcoats moved forward in a traditional battle line, but the outnumbered Americans were massed on a short front and delivered a withering fire. One-third of the attacking force fell while the Americans casualties were few. Shocked at their losses, the British left the field and sailed away. It was a triumphant end for the American nation and a reason to claim it had won the war.

American prestige rose throughout the world and the peace with England would be long lasting. America remained intact despite the pressure to break apart. James Madison had guided the disunited republic to victory and the liberties of the people under the Constitution had survived.

Return of the Barbary Pirates

When Madison was Secretary of State for Thomas Jefferson, he sent warships to the Mediterranean and forced a treaty on the Barbary pirates that American ships and sailors would not be attacked. While Madison's attention was on the War of 1812, Algiers ignored its agreement and captured an American ship and took the crew captive.

Nothing could be done during the war. Once the Treaty of Ghent was concluded, Congress declared war against Algiers and President Madison sent warships to rescue the American sailors. Ships from England and the Netherlands joined in the force to subdue the pirate governments and the long accepted system of appeasement by paying "tribute" was ended.

Death of Madison

James Madison outlived those who served with him in the momentous Convention of 1787 and became the voice of those past days, leaving his notes as the authority for that great debate.

It was their mutual belief in religious toleration and restraint of government power that had united the young Madison with Thomas Jefferson. From their political alliance grew an enduring personal bond. In his last days, Jefferson was to write to Madison of the "friendship which has subsisted between us, now half a century, and the harmony of our political principles and pursuits...".

After Jefferson's death, Madison noted that, "for a period of 50 years, during which there has not been an interruption or diminution of mutual confidence and cordial friendship, for a single moment in a single instance."

For the next eight years Madison served as the Rector of the University of Virginia, the last of the three Virginia presidents who had laid its cornerstone in 1817.

Madison was a semi-invalid during the last three years of his life, slowly sinking into death. He refused the stimulants which might have prolonged his life to July 4. Jefferson had died in 1826 and James Monroe in 1831, both on the Fourth of July.

Just six days short of that date, on June 26, 1836, Madison's niece asked, "What is the matter, Uncle Jeames," to which he replied, "Nothing more than a change of mind, my dear." With those last words, his death ended the Virginia Dynasty.

Dolley led the funeral possession to the family graveyard below Montpelier. Dolley would die in 1849 and her remains were removed from Congressional Cemetery in Washington in 1858 to lie beside her husband in the Madison Family Cemetery.

The United States after the war of 1812

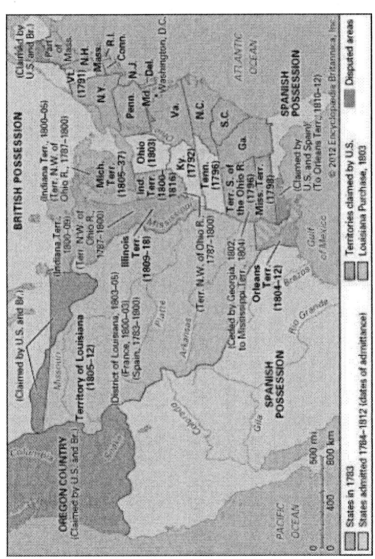

Credit: Encyclopædia Britannica, Inc.

JAMES MONROE

The Fifth President

Birthplace: Westmoreland County

Date of Birth: April 28, 1758

Term: March 4, 1817 – March 3, 1825

Vice President: David D. Tompkins
                                    1817-1825

Date of Death: July 4, 1831

Burial Place: Hollywood Cemetery
                                    Richmond

He left college to fight in the Revolutionary War and came back to forge, with Jefferson and Madison, a country securely in the hands of its people, safe from foreign intervention.

Early Years

The first Monroe came from the highlands of Scotland in 1665 and settled on the northern neck, that long peninsula of Virginia framed by the Potomac and the Rappahannock Rivers. He built **Monroe Hall** (Monrovia) on Monroe Creek where it enters the Potomac. Four generations later, James Monroe was born there on April 28, 1758, the oldest of five children. His father was Spence Monroe and his mother was Elizabeth Jones from King George County.

Monroe Hall had 500 acres used to raise cattle and grow tobacco, corn and barley, and Monroe's father could afford to send him to Campbelltown Academy for six years. When his father died in 1774, Monroe's uncle Joseph Jones, convinced him to attend the College of William & Mary in Williamsburg.

College Years

Monroe entered William & Mary in 1774 and was present in Williamsburg when Governor Dunmore tried to dissolve the General Assembly. It adjourned to the Raleigh Tavern and rallied the colonies to organize the first Continental Congress. The next year Dunmore sent British marines to seize a small store of powder in the magazine belonging to the city of Williamsburg. A call went out for militia units, one of which was led by Patrick Henry, to come to the capital and recapture the powder.

Next came Patrick Henry's electrifying speech at St. John's Episcopal Church in Richmond, "Give me liberty or give me death." This was all too much for the young Monroe and filled with revolutionary fire he left school to join the militia.

He was part of an advance guard that crossed the Delaware River in Washington's daring 1776 Christmas Day attack on Trenton. Severely wounded, Monroe returned to Virginia to recuperate. Promoted to major, he tried to raise a regiment but was unsuccessful. He rejoined Washington's army and participated in the Battle of Monmouth.

Monroe Hall
Birthplace of James Monroe

Major Andrew Monroe acquired the land in Westmoreland County in 1650 on which he built Monrovia, also known as Monroe Hall. James Monroe was born at Monroe Hall, a working plantation, which had about 500 acres in cattle, tobacco, corn and barley. The home in which Monroe was born was dismantled in the mid 1800's, but the outline of the house is laid out and there is a stone memorial marker. The land is owned by Westmoreland County.

Visitors: The site can be visited at any time.

Directions: The site is located on Virginia Route 205 in Westmoreland County. Go south from Fredericksburg on Virginia Route 3 to the intersection of Virginia Route 205 at Oak Grove and turn north on Route 205. A State Historical marker can be found 1.8 miles south of Colonial Beach.

109

Armed with a recommendation by Washington he went back to Virginia to obtain a post in the state forces but none was available. Encouraged by Thomas Jefferson, Monroe re-entered William & Mary to study law. When the capital was moved to Richmond in 1780, Jefferson, then Governor of Virginia, encouraged Monroe to continue his studies there and offered to be his mentor.

Shortly afterward, Cornwallis moved into Virginia and chased Jefferson and the General Assembly to Charlottesville. When Cornwallis moved toward Yorktown, Monroe tried again for a command. He applied to Lafayette but no officer posts were open.

By war's end the King George County member of the House of Delegates was James Monroe. Appointed as a delegate to the Confederation Congress in 1783, he lodged with Thomas Jefferson in Annapolis. There he met James Madison. The friendship of these three men would survive the turmoil of the next four decades as they led onto the world stage the young country they helped to create.

Monroe served in the Confederation Congress for three years. During this time he took two trips to visit the western states and became a strong supporter of American expansion.

Rising Politician

While a member of Congress in New York, Monroe met and married Elizabeth Kortright. He brought his young bride to Fredericksburg in 1786 and rented the *Joseph Jones House* from his uncle and resided there until 1789.
He opened a law office where the site of the *James Monroe Museum* is now located.

He was elected to the Virginia General Assembly, and he was upset that he was not selected the following year as a delegate to the Constitutional Convention meeting in Philadelphia. When the Virginia Convention met for the ratification of the new Constitution, Monroe joined forces with Patrick Henry and George Mason. They opposed ratification of the Constitution because it was not subject to a bill of rights. James Madison convinced the Convention that if it ratified the Constitution the new Congress would adopt a bill of rights.

The next year, Patrick Henry talked Monroe into running for Congress against Madison. Monroe's motive is unclear, since Madison had promised the Virginia Convention he would seek a bill of rights in the new Congress. Madison won easily over Monroe and the event did not harm the friendship between the two men.

First Mission to France

Thomas Jefferson returned from France in 1789 and accepted the offer of George Washington to become Secretary of State. At Jefferson's encouragement, Monroe purchased 800 acres in Charlottesville which he called his "lower plantation." Today, it is known as **Monroe Hill** on the campus of the University of Virginia. Several years later he purchased land a short distance from Monticello which he named "Highland." Today, it is called **Ash Lawn-Highland.** His efforts at farming the lower plantation were unsuccessful. The debt he incurred was the start of financial difficulties that would last to the end of his life.

War between England and France soon divided Washington's cabinet. Federalists, led by Alexander Hamilton, sided with England. The anti-federalists (or Jeffersonian republicans) felt a strong obligation to the French for their

---

Joseph Jones House

Joseph Jones served in the Revolution and was friends with George Washington and Thomas Jefferson. He was an uncle and surrogate father to James Monroe. After Monroe's marriage in 1786 to Elizabeth Kortright, the young couple came to Fredericksburg where Monroe intended to practice law. Jones had just built a house at 301 Caroline Street which Monroe rented from 1786-1789. It was a two story brick house with two attached porches. It had two small outbuildings, one a kitchen. Shortly before the Civil War, the house was raised to three stories and the brick was covered with stucco. The side and rear additions were built in the late 1900s. The home is privately owned and is not open to the public.

James Monroe Museum

After the Revolutionary War, James Monroe practiced law in Fredericksburg, Virginia, from 1786 to 1789. The James Monroe Museum is located approximately where his law office once stood. Many important items associated with Monroe are in the Museum including the Louis XVI desk on which Monroe prepared his annual message to Congress in 1823 and set out the principles of the Monroe Doctrine. The Museum also contains a memorial library with thousands of books and historical manuscripts related to Monroe. A bronze bust of James Monroe by Margaret French Cresson is in the garden. The Museum is owned by the Commonwealth of Virginia and is administered by Mary Washington College.

Visitors: The Museum is open from 10:00 a.m. to 5:00 p.m. Monday thru Saturday and from 1:00 p.m. to 5:00 p.m. on Sunday, except December, January and February, when the closing time is 4:00 p.m.. Closed Thanksgiving Day, Christmas Day and New Year's Day. After the guided tour, you may re-visit the galleries on a self-guided tour. Visit the Museum shop for unique gifts of the Revolutionary period.

Directions: The Museum is located on Charles Street in the historic city of Fredericksburg. Drive into Fredericksburg from Interstate 95 (Exit 130A) and follow Virginia Route 3 (William Street), Business Route, past Mary Washington College, to Charles Street, then turn right and follow the signs to the historic area.

Contact: James Monroe Museum and Memorial Library, 908 Charles Street, Fredericksburg, Virginia 22401-5810; (540) 654-1043; JamesMonroeMuseum.umw.edu

A bronze bust of James Monroe by Margaret French Cresson stands in the garden of the James Monroe Museum

112

timely support of America during the Revolutionary War.

Washington struggled to keep the United States neutral and he asked Monroe to accept the post of Minister to France. Although Monroe had risen to a leadership position in the U. S. Senate, he accepted Washington's offer. Washington wanted someone sympathetic to the French people, but Monroe was charged by the Federalists as too pro-French. Finally, after two years, Washington asked him to return.

James Monroe assumed the life of a farmer and lawyer on his Charlottesville plantation. He hoped his second property — Highland — would be a permanent home and the lands would provide an income for his old age. It was only a short time, however, before public service, in which he would spend most of his life, beckoned again. In 1799, Monroe was elected governor of Virginia for the first of three one year terms.

Monroe and Slavery

Added to the white fear engendered by the bloody revolt in Haiti in the 1790s, Monroe faced his own rebellion as governor of Virginia in 1800. Hundreds of slaves were

Monroe Hill

James Monroe received Kentucky lands for his service in the Continental Army. These parcels he traded in 1788 for an 800 acre plantation and house in Charlottesville, which he called the "lower plantation." Monroe built two one story brick buildings, one for a home and the other for his law office. It is unclear whether Monroe ever lived on the property. He tried to make it a working plantation but it was never profitable, so he sold the property about 1806. A portion was purchased about 1820 for the new University of Virginia. Eventually, all of the property was acquired for the University. The law office is the only building on the campus that pre-dates Jefferson's "academical village." An arcade built in the mid 1800's now connects the law office to a building erected on the site of Monroe's original home. Portions of Monroe's home survive in the dining room and basement meeting room of the current building. Located on a slight rise above on McCormick Road, the buildings are now part of Brown College.

The Story of Ash Lawn—Highland

James Monroe bought 1,000 acres in 1793 in Albemarle County before he left to become Minister to France. He had selected the site at the urging of Thomas Jefferson who wanted to create a "society to our taste" in Albemarle County. It was first called the "Upper Plantation" to distinguish it from the "Lower Plantation," land owned by Monroe in Charlottesville. Later, it was referred to more formally as "Highlands" or "Highland." Monroe continued to acquire tracts until the plantation grew to 3,400 acres. In 1799, he built a small house and worked the plantation except for the period 1803-1807 when he was a special envoy to France and England. In 1811, he became Madison's Secretary of State and moved to Washington. Although he returned annually to Highland, his political obligations and his election as president prevented his close supervision of the farm. He tried to sell but was caught in a severe depression of real estate values throughout Virginia. He insisted the price must indemnify him for the "sacrifice" of his residence of twenty-six years. It was not until 1826 that he managed to sell the dwelling house and nine hundred acres. He eventually surrendered the remaining 2800 acres to eliminate the debt owed the bank. After the property was purchased by Alexander Garrett in 1837, the plantation was renamed Ash Lawn. The Massey family purchased Ash Lawn just after the Civil War and erected an addition on the front of the original house. Jay Winston Johns purchased the house and 630 3/4 acres in 1930 and bequeathed it to the College of William & Mary, the school which Monroe had left to fight in the Revolutionary War. Johns' will required the College to operate the "property as an historic shrine for the general education of the public." William & Mary restored the name Highland — so long forgotten — and opened the home to the public in 1985.

Visitors: Ash Lawn-Highland is open daily from 9:00 a.m. to 6:00 p.m. April thru October, and from 11:00 a.m. to 5:00 p.m. November thru March, and is closed Thanksgiving Day, Christmas Day and New Year's Day.

Directions: Ash Lawn-Highland is south of Charlottesville, Virginia on Va. Route 795. Follow the signs from Interstate 64. It is a short distance from Monticello on Virginia Route 53 to Virginia Route 795. There is a gift shop.

Contact: Ash Lawn-Highland, 2050 James Monroe Parkway, Charlottesville, Virginia 22902; (434) 293-8000; www.ashlawnhighland.org/

part of the uprising, but it became known by its leader as *Gabriel's Conspiracy*. Although it did not change Monroe's attitude that slavery should be abolished, it influenced his belief that assimilation of the enslaved community was not possible in the United States.

When he was president, Monroe supported a deportation plan for free blacks to a country that was acquired for that purpose in Africa, later called Liberia (from Latin for "free"). The capital city was named Monrovia in his honor.

Gabriel's Conspiracy

It was during Monroe's governorship that a major slave revolt occurred. Led by Gabriel, a slave on the Thomas Prosser plantation, the conspirators secretly prepared swords and bullets through the spring of 1800. This activity created some suspicion and Monroe was warned about the possibility of an uprising. Two slaves revealed the plot the day before it was to occur and Monroe called out the militia. A part of the plan was to capture rifles stored in Richmond and to kidnap Monroe. That night approximately 1000 slaves met at the rendezvous point, but a tremendous thunderstorm had flooded a low area and blocked the road to Richmond. Most of the slaves drifted back to their plantations. Over the next several days, hundreds of blacks were arrested, and approximately 35 were eventually executed. Although the conspiracy may have included hundreds of other slaves in adjoining counties, Monroe was cautious about retaliation. Jefferson advised him that Virginia could not "indulge a principle of revenge," and a number of those held were freed. Monroe believed that slavery was contrary to nature and should be abolished. Although Virginia had permitted manumission since 1782, there was strong public opposition to freeing those who were unable to support themselves. There was great concern as to how the former African slave could be integrated into the white society, both from a social dynamic and an economic adjustment. Part of Gabriel's plan was to slaughter the white population. Years before, Jefferson had expressed his concern that freedom of the slaves would lead to "the extermination of the one or the other race."

Second Mission to France

After his election as president in 1800, Thomas Jefferson sent James Monroe to France to acquire the port at New Orleans from Napoleon. Jefferson instructed Monroe to "defend the future destinies of this Republic." When Monroe arrived in France he found that Napoleon was willing to sell the entire Louisiana Territory. Monroe's long association with Jefferson gave the French confidence that Monroe had the authority to negotiate the terms.

Back in the United States, Jefferson and his Secretary of State, James Madison, were concerned that the Constitution did not authorize this purchase but no one in the Congress raised the constitutional objection. Monroe's purchase more than doubled the territory of the United States.

While Monroe was in France, Napoleon's war with England threatened America's right to the open seas. British war ships stopped American merchant ships, removed American seamen and forced them into service in the British navy. James Madison asked Monroe to go to England and negotiate a treaty of commerce which would also end the impressment of American sailors.

Monroe was pleased with the terms he obtained from Great Britain. However, because he failed to reach an agreement to end impressment Jefferson did not submit the treaty to the Congress. Monroe returned with the unhappy feeling that all his efforts on the treaty had been wasted.

Secretary of State

James Madison had been a political ally of Thomas Jefferson for over thirty years and his Secretary of State during both of Jefferson's terms. Madison was the natural choice of the republicans to succeed Jefferson as president. However, "old republican" groups in Virginia felt Madison was weak on states rights and promoted James Monroe.

Monroe was still upset that his efforts on the trade treaty in 1806 had not been appreciated by Jefferson and Madison. Although Monroe did not campaign, he allowed his name to be used. He got no electoral votes and put his political alliance with Madison in jeopardy.

Madison easily defeated his Federalist opponent and he held no resentment for Monroe's opposition. The new president erased their past differences by appointing Monroe as Secretary of State. The most crucial foreign policy issue continued to be the great conflict between England and Napoleon. James Monroe tried to follow the policy first set by George Washington to steer a neutral course.

Finally, the violations by the British against American ships exhausted the patience of the young "war hawks" in Congress. Behind their patriotic fervor, President Madison took the young nation into the War of 1812.

Dissatisfied with the efforts of the War Department, Monroe assumed the duties of the Secretary of War along with those of Secretary of State. His efforts helped guide America to victory and international recognition.

First Term

Some Federalists were still around in 1816, but the Federalist party had disappeared. Jeffersonian Republicans were in complete control. Republican members of Congress nominated James Monroe for president and he won all but three states.

Perhaps influenced by George Washington's grand tour, Monroe was anxious to explore the United States. His first trip through the northeast and northwest states was at the beginning of his presidency. Several years later he traveled down the east coast and selected the site of Fortress Monroe. From Savannah, he turned north to Tennessee and finally eastward to Lexington and on to his home in Albemarle County. He was popular in the western territories whose interests were often overlooked by the eastern states.

He also sent out military and scientific expeditions to explore the west and establish military forts. Although none received the same acclaim as the Lewis and Clark expedition, they kept Americans excited about the great expanse that stretched from the Mississippi River to the Pacific Ocean.

As the settlers moved west, tension with the Indian tribes increased. President Monroe felt more strongly than Thomas Jefferson or James Madison that the treaties with the Indians should be respected. This was soon tested when the Seminoles attacked American settlements in Florida.

England had ceded Florida to Spain after the Revolutionary War. Monroe did not hesitate to send Andrew Jackson to put down the Seminole revolt. Spain protested but backed away from a conflict with America. Spain feared that the U. S. also had designs on Mexico, so surrendered Florida to avoid a war.

At the end of James Monroe's first term, slavery again challenged the intent of the Founding Fathers. When Missouri petitioned to become a state, opposition arose in Congress over its admission unless the state agreed to ban slavery. Monroe felt that such a restriction on Missouri would be unconstitutional. In a letter to Jefferson, President Monroe wrote he had "never known a question so menacing to the tranquility and even the continuance of our Union..."

The issue of disunion was avoided by the **Missouri Compromise** to admit Missouri as a slave state and Maine as a free state and to ban slavery in any future state north of a western extension of Missouri's southern border.

Second Term

In his second bid for the presidency, James Monroe faced no opposition. Jeffersonian republicanism united the country and Monroe received all but one electoral vote. Although the president was head of the executive branch, presidential authority was not defined in the Constitution. Most of the functions of government were assigned to the Congress. President Monroe was reminded of this when Congress rejected some of his military nominations. He even found it necessary to caution cabinet members to follow his directions and policy.

Despite the struggle over presidential power, Monroe faced no domestic or international problems. The country continued to expand on a wave of national optimism. Mon

Missouri Compromise

In 1818, Missouri applied to the Congress to be admitted to the Union as a state. This area was part of the Louisiana Territory which James Monroe had negotiated to purchase from Napoleon in 1803. Slavery had existed throughout the Louisiana Territory before it was acquired by the United States. Opposition arose over the admission of Missouri as a slave state. It was argued that the Founding Fathers did not intend the extension of slavery beyond the original states, since Congress had banned slavery in the Northwest Territory in 1787. Up to this time, slavery had been a state issue, not a condition for admission to the Union. By tradition, new states had been admitted with the same privileges as the original states. Anti-slavery groups in free states raised the threat of secession. At this time, the northern portion of Massachusetts sought admission as the new state of Maine. This provided a compromise to admit Missouri with no restrictions on slavery, and Maine as a free state. The balance in the Union would be kept equal — twelve slave and twelve free. It was agreed that future states carved from the rest of the Louisiana Territory above the north latitude line of 36° 36' (Missouri's southern border) would be free. Thomas Jefferson thought the opposition of the northern states to Missouri a "fire bell in the night." To him, it was "the knell of the Union. It is hushed, indeed," he wrote, "for the moment, but this is a reprieve only, not a final sentence."

roe's presidency came to be known as the "era of good feelings."

Monroe Doctrine

When Napoleon conquered Spain, the Spanish colonies in the Americas revolted and became independent. A number of European countries—loosely organized as the Holy Alliance— wanted to restore Spanish rule. At the same time, the claim of the United States to its Pacific northwest was being contested by Russia. England at first supported the United States, but Monroe decided the country should stand alone against any European intervention in the Americas.

His time as president was drawing to a close when he sent to Congress on December 2, 1823, the president's annual message. He reaffirmed the policy established by George Washington that the United States would not interfere in European affairs. The "American continents," he declared were not "subjects for future colonization" by the European powers. Monroe warned that any attempt to extend a European political system to the western hemisphere was dangerous to the "peace and safety of the United States." Thomas Jefferson termed the issue "momentous."

It was a bold move by Monroe to tell the powers of Europe what their foreign policy should be toward the Americas. He was not backed up by an act of Congress and his warning of non-intervention did not become international law. The principles laid out by Monroe did become a statement of the American attitude. Over the next one hundred years, American foreign policy would be based on the Monroe Doctrine.

Last days

Like his predecessors, Jefferson and Madison, James Monroe was deeply in debt when he completed his second term as president. He had tried for a number of years to sell either the Highland or the *Oak Hill* properties. With the proceeds, he would eliminate his debts and improve the other estate for his retirement.

A deepening depression in land values in Virginia made that impossible. When the Marquis de Lafayette visited the United States in 1825, he applied to the Congress of the United States for compensation for his efforts in the Revolution fifty years before. Monroe was very supportive of this request and Lafayette received a $200,000 grant from the Congress, plus land in Florida.

When Monroe sought compensation for the balance of his services, which had never been fully paid, there was opposition in the Congress and he received barely enough to cover his outstanding bills. He lost the Highland property when he could not pay the mortgage and was forced to turn it over to the bank.

Monroe faced all of this with his usual stoic but kind demeanor. Another tragedy struck when his wife of thirty-

The Story of Oak Hill

James Monroe purchased this property in Loudoun County with his uncle and became sole owner on his uncle's death in 1805. He used the six room cottage as a place to escape from Washington during the time he was Secretary of State and President. He stayed in what became the overseer's house and continued to make improvements until 1820 when he began to build the current home in anticipation of his retirement. Constructed of brick with two wings, he received design suggestions by letter from Thomas Jefferson. The oak trees, which gave the estate its name, one for each state in the union, supposedly were donated by members of Congress. After Monroe left the presidency, he retired to Oak Hill to farm and tried to rebuild his finances. A depression in Virginia land prices made it impossible for Monroe to sell either his home Highland in Albemarle County or Oak Hill. Because of the death of his wife in 1830 and his own failing health he went to New York to live with his daughter, Maria, to whom he left Oak Hill. The property was sold in 1852 to John Walton Fairfax and was used as his private residence. A later owner enlarged the end rooms and added porticos in 1922. Other than these improvements, the home remains essentially as constructed by Monroe. Located on Virginia Route 15 south of Leesburg, it remains a private residence and is not open to the public. Unfortunately, large trees make it impossible to view from the road.

four years, who suffered from an undisclosed fainting ailment, fell near an open fire at Oak Hill and was grievously burned She died three years later.

There seemed little left for him in Virginia, so he deeded Oak Hill to his daughter, Maria, and in September, 1830, left to live out the last few months of his life with her in New York City.

Death and Burial

James Monroe died on July 4, 1831. Incredibly, out of the first five presidents, he was the third, along with John Adams and Thomas Jefferson, to die on the day of American Independence.

Throughout the towns and cities of America, James

Monroe's great contributions were remembered. On the military posts, guns fired his last salute. He had remained to the end of his life as Thomas Jefferson once described him: "You could turn his soul wrong side outwards and there would be not a speck on it."

His funeral possession passed down Broadway to his burial in the Second Street Cemetery. In 1858, his remains were returned to Virginia and were buried in Hollywood Cemetery in Richmond

---

Hollywood Cemetery

Situated on the banks of the James River, Hollywood Cemetery in Richmond, Virginia was designed in 1847. It is one of America's most beautiful "garden cemeteries." All nationalities, religions and races are buried there. The remains of James Monroe, fifth president of the United States, were re-interred in Hollywood Cemetery in 1858. John Tyler, the tenth president of the United States, was buried there in 1862.

Visitors: Hollywood Cemetery is open daily Monday to Friday from 8:00 a.m. to 5:00 p.m., and 6:00 p.m. during daylight saving time. There are historical walking tours Monday through Saturday from April through October at 10:00 a.m. Meet your guide at the Cemetery entrance at Cherry and Albemarle Streets; call (804) 649-0711 Ext. 334

Directions: See the detailed instructions on reaching Hollywood Cemetery from multiple starting points http://www.hollywoodcemetery.org/directions.html

Contact: Hollywood Cemetery Company, 412 South Cherry Street, Richmond, VA 23220; (804) 648-8501; http://www.hollywoodcemetery.org/index.html

The United States after the Missouri Compromise of 1820

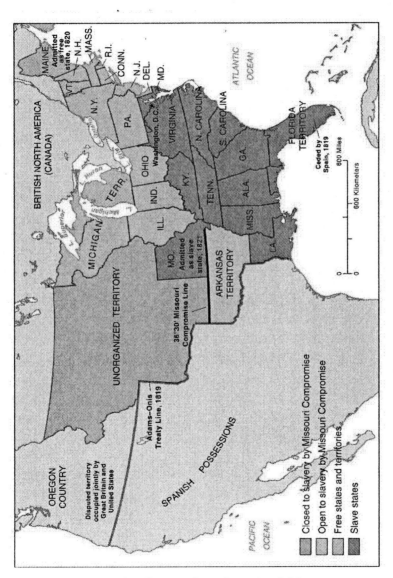

Credit: teachers.henrico.k12.va.us

William Henry Harrison

The Ninth President

Birthplace: Berkeley Plantation

Date of Birth: February 9, 1773

Term: March 4, 1841—April 4, 1841

Vice President: John Tyler 1841

Date of Death: April 4, 1841

Burial Place: Harrison Tomb

North Bend, Ohio

He challenged the frontier in America's move west.

Early Years

Benjamin Harrison V was a speaker of the Virginia General Assembly, Governor of Virginia and a signer of the Declaration of Independence. He descended from one of Virginia's oldest families and grew to inherit Berkeley, one of the grand homes on the James River. In 1748, he married Elizabeth Bassett and they had seven children.

The last child was William Henry Harrison, born February 9, 1773, on the eve of the Revolutionary War. He was old enough to see the traitor Benedict Arnold's raid on *Berkeley* when Redcoats burned family pictures, furniture and clothes, shot the cattle and took the horses.

Harrison enrolled in Hampton-Sydney College in 1787 to study medicine. When Benjamin V became aware his son had joined an abolitionist society, he sent him to Philadelphia to study at the Medical School of Pennsylvania University. Benjamin V died suddenly. Like many who fought for

Berkeley
Birthplace of William Henry Harrison

A group of merchants, granted a charter by the Virginia Company, sent the ship *Margaret* to Virginia with thirty-five settlers. It landed on December 4, 1619 on the north shore of the James River at the site of what would become known as Berkeley Hundred. About 8,000 acres in size, the site was "more towards west and Sherley Hundred, and toward Charles Ciity." The original town only lasted a few years when an Indian massacre in 1622 brought an end to the settlement. The land was acquired in 1691 by Benjamin Harrison II. Named for Richard Berkeley, one of the original leaders of that first landing, the house was built in 1726 by Benjamin Harrison IV, near the original landing site. His son, Benjamin Harrison V, born at Berkeley during the year the house was completed, became a signer of the Declaration of Independence, and governor of Virginia (1781-1784) during the final years of the Revolutionary War. Berkeley was the birth place and boyhood home of the ninth president, William Henry Harrison, the third son of Benjamin V. Two generations later, Benjamin Harrison, grandson of William Henry Harrison, became the nation's twenty-third president. Scottish immigrant John Jamieson was a drummer boy with the Union army and camped at Berkeley (then called Harrison's Landing) during the Civil War. He bought the property in the early 1900's but it remained in a run down condition until inherited by his son. In the 1930's, Malcolm and Grace Jamieson began the restoration which returned the house to its former grandeur. This Georgian mansion is reputed to be the oldest brick home in America. It is now owned by Malcolm E. Jamieson and his family.

Visitors: Berkeley is open daily from 10:30 a.m. to 3:30 p.m. January to mid-March and open daily mid-March through December from 9:30 a.m. to 4:30 p.m. There are guided tours for the house. Tours of the gardens are self-guided. There is a gift shop.

Directions: Berkeley is located 25 miles from Williamsburg west on Virginia Route 5. From I-295 it is 15 miles east on Virginia Route 5.

Contact: Berkeley, 12602 Harrison Landing Road, Charles City, Virginia 23030; (804) 829-6018 or (888) 466-6018; www.berkeleyplantation.com

independence, he left his estate mired in debt. Tobacco had exhausted the soil at Berkeley. The great plantation, where America celebrated its *first Thanksgiving,* could not support his son's education.

William Harrison decided to pursue a military career. With his name and connections, he soon obtained a commission in the army and was on his way to the frontier at Fort Pitt.

First Thanksgiving

The ceremony of thanks given by the immigrants at Berkeley Hundred was the first Thanksgiving in America. The settlers were instructed "that the day of our ships arrival at the place assigned for plantation in the land of Virginia shall be yearly and perpetually kept holy as a day of thanksgiving to Almighty God." Upon landing, all knelt and prayed. Today, a brick gazebo at Berkeley marks the site with the inscribed words of the instruction. A Virginia statute (§ 2.2-3300) officially established "The Fourth Thursday in November and the Friday next following Thanksgiving Day to honor and give thanks in each person's own manner for the blessings bestowed upon the people of Virginia and honoring the first Thanksgiving in 1619."

Soldier

When the Treaty of Paris in 1783 ended the French and Indian War, American settlers moved into the area north of the Ohio River. Congress passed the Northwest Ordinance in 1787, creating the territory out of which would come the states of Ohio, Indiana, Illinois, Wisconsin and portions of Minnesota. Native tribes had long occupied this territory and they fought to keep it. The settlers called for the army to protect them from Indian retaliation.

In one of his first acts as president, George Washington sent American militia to clear out Indian resistance to white settlement in the Northwest Territory. Poorly trained, the Americans suffered substantial casualties and were forced to retreat in the Battle of the Wabash on November 4, 1790.

Four years later, President Washington sent a larger

force. General Anthony Wayne defeated the Miami under Chief Little Turtle at the Battle of Fallen Timbers and chased what remained of the tribe into Canada. This forced almost one hundred chiefs to sign the Treaty of Fort Greeneville and cede to the United States an area which later became Ohio and most of Indiana.

Wayne's young aide in the battle was William Henry Harrison. Harrison had shown Wayne and the men under his command that he would be an outstanding soldier. Lieutenant Harrison was assigned the duty of enforcing the terms of the treaty with the Indians.

Marriage

On a military mission to Kentucky, William Henry Harrison met Anna Tuthill Symmes, the daughter of a judge in the Indiana Territory. However, the career of an army officer was not what the judge expected for his daughter's husband. When Harrison asked for her hand, Judge Symmes refused, so while he was away the young couple were married on November 25, 1795.

Judge Symmes accepted the union and sold Harrison a log cabin for their first home, near the Ohio River in North Bend. They would eventually have ten children and the "log cabin" would become famous in Harrison's campaign for president.

Political Beginning

Although he was promoted to captain after his performance at Fallen Timbers, Harrison was pessimistic about his future in the army and resigned. He soon received an appointment as Secretary of the Northwest Territory from President Adams. Under the terms of the Northwest Ordinance, once the territory reached a certain population it was entitled to a representative in Congress. Harrison ran for the post and won.

In 1800, the Division Act divided the Northwest Territory. Several years later the eastern part was admitted to the Union as the State of Ohio. The western part, out of which would come the states of Indiana, Illinois and Wisconsin,

Michigan and a portion of Minnesota, was now the Indiana Territory. Its new governor, appointed by the president, was the 28 year old William Henry Harrison.

Under Harrison's authority was a vast area without roads. Most of it was *Indian land*. There were many tribes and they roamed all across the frontier. It had never been a policy of the English colonists to absorb the Indians.

President Jefferson conceived a plan to turn these indigenous natives into farmers but they would not change their way of life. It was up to Governor Harrison to convince the Indians to cede their land to the U. S. and to move to a new territory. This was a pattern that would be repeated as these Indian tribes were pushed westward.

Indian Land

When Great Britain established its American colonies, the indigenous natives were considered a conquered people with no claim to the land. After the Revolution, the Americans recognized that the Indians had a claim to "the soil they possessed." When the Constitution was adopted in 1788, it did not recognize native peoples as citizens. They were a "domestic dependent nation" on United States land. To the indians, land over which the tribe hunted was "Indian land." Sometimes the hunting areas overlapped and which tribe occupied the land was not always clear. Once the United States obtained a treaty, it generally refused to recognize the claims of any other tribes to the same land. When the tribe agreed to cede their land to the U. S., they were given some compensation and a new location. Tribes that refused to move and resisted were forced from their land by the U. S. Army. Those tribes who would not cede their "land" in the Northwest Territory were forced out by William Henry Harrison in 1810-1813. President James Monroe authorized Andrew Jackson to subdue the Seminoles in Florida in 1816. Zachary Taylor, then a colonel in the U. S. Army, fought in the Black Hawk war in 1832, and in 1837 commanded the American forces in the Second Seminole War. By 1890, virtually all the land in the U S. was covered by an Indian cession treaty. It was not until 1924 that U. S. citizenship was granted to these Native Americans.

Battle of Tippecanoe

In 1809, Harrison negotiated the Treaty of Fort Wayne to acquire millions of acres covering the future states of Illinois and southern Indiana. Angered by the treaty, a Shawnee chief, *Tecumseh,* wrote a letter to Governor Harrison. Tecumseh claimed that the land was owned by all Indians and could not be sold unless all tribes agreed. Harrison invited him to *Grouseland* but the meeting went badly. Tecumseh was adamant that the land treaty was not binding on the Indians and that the white man had no right to take the land.

Tecumseh tried to convince all the tribes, from the Indiana Territory to Louisiana, to form an Alliance to fight the takeover of Indian land. Faced with an uprising, President Madison appointed Governor Harrison to take command of the military force.

Although Madison told Harrison not to provoke a war, Harrison believed the Indians were planning an attack. When he received information that Tecumseh was away, Harrison took about 1000 men and marched on Prophetstown, the Alliance capital, where the Tippecanoe Creek flows into the Wabash River. Harrison prepared camp near the town and was careful to establish his pickets and sentinels.

Led by Tecumseh's brother, Tenskwatawa, also known as the Prophet, the Indians struck before dawn on November 11, 1811. Harrison cooly repulsed repeated attacks. Finally, the Indians refused to continue the fight. Promised a great victory, they felt the Prophet had failed them and many tribes drifted west. Upon Tecumseh's return, he began to rebuild Prophetstown and the Alliance.

Battle of the Thames

After the Revolution, the English continued to treat America as a second rate power. American ships were stopped on the high seas and American sailors taken off to be impressed in the British navy. Presidents Washington and Jefferson did not have a navy that could fight back.

Finally, in Madison's presidency, the War Hawks in Congress could take no more abuse from England and is-

Tecumseh

Tecumseh was born in 1768, the son of a Shawnee chief. After his father's death he was taken to Alabama. He later returned to the Northwest Territory and fought at the Battle of Fallen Timbers. When William Henry Harrison negotiated the Treaty of Fort Wayne with the Indians, Tecumseh refused to sign for his tribe. Along with his brother Tenskwatawa, called the Prophet, he began preaching to the tribes that they were all "children of the same parents." No chief could cede land to the United States because it was owned in common by all Indians. Tecumseh traveled as far south as Georgia and Alabama to organize a confederation of all the tribes. They were drawn together by the vision of the Prophet that the Great Spirit would restore the Indian world. Their capital was a settlement on the Tippecanoe River, which the whites called Prophetstown. In 1811, the Indian Alliance was shattered at the Battle of Tippecanoe in western Indiana when William Henry Harrison, in Tecumseh's absence, routed the tribes and burned Prophetstown. The next year, Tecumseh fought with the British in the War of 1812 believing they would help stop the American's advance in the Northwest Territory. He was killed on October 5, 1813, at the Battle of the Thames. With him died the vision of joining all the tribes in a great confederation.

sued a declaration of war on June 18, 1812. Tecumseh saw another chance to stop the American settlers. Along with his brother he joined with the English to occupy Detroit.

President Madison made Harrison commander-in-chief of the Army of the Northwest, made up of both militia and regular units. After the British fleet was driven from the Great Lakes by Oliver Hazard Perry, Harrison retook Detroit.

He pursued the British army and their Indian allies into Canada. On October 15, 1813, he caught up with them at the Thames River. When the English lines broke and were driven from the field, Tecumseh refused to retreat and was slain. The vision of a great Indian Alliance died with him.

Campaign for President

William Henry Harrison left the army after the War of 1812 and served in the House of Representatives and Senate. He was sent to Colombia in 1828 as minister but was

The Story of Grouseland

William Henry Harrison constructed Grouseland (1803-04) during the time he was governor of the Indiana Territory. It was on the edge of civilization and was built like a fort. Located on the Wabash River in Vincennes on what was then the Indiana Territory, the outer brick walls were 18 inches thick with slits as portholes to fire through. A powder magazine was located in the cellar. Harrison's large family remained in the house until 1812, when he moved them to his farm in North Bend, Ohio. It stayed in the family until 1850. It was rescued from destruction in 1909 when it was purchased by the Francis Vigo Chapter of the Daughters of the American Revolution. The house has been carefully restored and has been opened to the public as an historic house museum since 1911. It is supported by admissions, sales of souvenirs and contributions.

Visitors: Open daily March through December from 10:00 a.m. to 5:00 p.m.; and January – February from 11:00 a.m. to 4:00 p.m., except Mondays; also closed Thanksgiving Day, Christmas Day and New Year's Day

Directions: Minutes from Highway 41 east of Vincennes. Turn West onto Hart Street; turn right onto 1st Street; cross rail road tracks and turn left on Scott Street; Grouseland will be on your right.

Contact: Grouseland, 3 West Scott Street, Vincennes, Indiana 47591; (812)882-2096; www.grouselandfoundation.org/index.html

critical of the dictatorial powers assumed by Simón Bolivar.

Recalled by the United States, he returned to North Bend, Ohio in debt. He also took on the added burden of restoring the fortunes of two of his sons. In May, 1836, he was fortunate to obtain an appointment as Hamilton County Clerk.

In that year, a new party called **Whigs** was formed. They were called many different names by the opposition because the party was a collection of anti-Jackson votes and single interest groups. There were three Whig candidates for president which split the vote and allowed Martin Van Buren to win. Harrison was one of the candidates as a favorite son of the western states.

Whigs

After James Monroe's two terms, the Federalist party slowly disintegrated. Many found a place in Henry Clay's American System, advocating issues of internal improvements and protective tariffs. But Clay's National Republicans had a major setback when the Democrat Andrew Jackson was elected president. Then Jackson threatened South Carolina with force if it resisted tariffs. Next, he withdrew government funds in order to shut down the national bank. This chased away many states-righters and Democrats. Some voters joined a party that opposed the influence of the Masons. All of these groups came together under the Whig party banner. The name was first used in England for Scottish dissenters and later for those who advocated the power of Parliament over the crown. The Whigs attracted competing interests of northern manufacturers, capitalists, southern cotton planters and abolitionists. It united behind William Henry Harrison, remembered for the battle that broke the Indian Alliance of Tecumseh, and made him the first president of the new party. Eight years later, in 1848, Zachary Taylor, hero of the Mexican War, was also elected president as a Whig. William Henry Harrison and Zachary Taylor, the only Virginia presidents to die in office, were the first and the last Whigs elected to the presidency. Sectional differences between north and south broke the Whigs apart in 1852 and it disappeared as a national party, many to find their way to the emerging Republican party.

Of the three candidates, Harrison most impressed the Whig voters and they united behind him in 1840. His views on some of the major issues, tariffs, slavery and anti-masonry, were vague. It made him the candidate best able to straddle the issues in a party of dissenters.

Tippecanoe and Tyler Too

In order to appeal to the southern states-righters and those concerned with tariffs, the Whigs chose John Tyler of Virginia as the vice-presidential candidate. Tyler was from Charles City County, Virginia, the same county in which William Henry Harrison was born. Both Harrison and Tyler came from the same aristocratic, planter background.

It was one of the most colorful campaigns in American history. Issues were ignored while slogans and name-calling took over the campaign. At first, the Democrats tried to make fun of Harrison as an old man in ill health, content to sit in his log cabin and drink hard cider (he had become a teetotaler). But the comment backfired when the Whigs promoted the log cabin, hard cider and the coonskin cap as symbols for the common man of the frontier. Many at that time came from log cabins.

Actually, Harrison's first house had been enlarged to sixteen rooms, although the family still called it the "log cabin." The voters were also reminded of Harrison's great victory over Tecumseh in the slogan, "Tippecanoe and Tyler too."

Although their native state, Virginia, rejected them, nineteen states gave Harrison and Tyler a decisive win. Harrison visited his boyhood home Berkeley and in his mother's old room wrote his inaugural address.

A sharp wind blew through Washington on inauguration day. Perhaps to show that his health was good, Harrison, hatless and coatless, remained outside in the cold for one and one half hours.

Death of Harrison

Three weeks later, Harrison was in bed with a fever. He was up after a week but quickly fell ill again. On April 4,

1841, he was dead. His last words: "Sir, I wish you to understand the true principles of government. I wish them carried out. I ask nothing more."

In the shortest term of any president, Harrison left no presidential legacy. He was awarded the highest office in America as one of the generation that surged westward in the decades before the Civil War and took America to the Pacific Ocean. His grandson, Benjamin Harrison, would become the nation's twenty-third president.

Gary Smith Images

Berkeley Plantation

One of the great James River plantations, it was the site of the first Thanksgiving in America, December 4, 1619, and is the ancestral home of two U. S. presidents, William Henry Harrison and his grandson, Benjamin Harrison.

JOHN TYLER

The Tenth President

Birthplace: Greenway

Date of Birth: March 29, 1790

Term: April 6, 1841—March 3, 1845

Vice President: None

Date of Death: January 18, 1862

Burial Place: Hollywood Cemetery

Richmond

He was the first vice-president to be elevated to the presidency and he established the principle of presidential succession that has been followed ever since.

Early years

The first Tyler was Henry and he came from England in the mid 1600s and settled at Middle Plantation (later to be called Williamsburg). The Tyler's prospered in Virginia and by the time of the future president's birth on March 29, 1790, his father was politically prominent and a substantial property owner.

Tyler was born at the plantation home, *Greenway*, on March 29, 1790, the second son and sixth child of his father's marriage to Mary Armistead. His mother died when Tyler was seven and the loss was severe but he was fortunate to have a caring father who raised not only Tyler and his siblings, but others for whom he was guardian.

The young John Tyler entered the preparatory school at the *College of William & Mary* when he was twelve and completed his studies at the college at seventeen. While in school, he resided at the *James Semple House*. After graduation, Tyler began to read for the law under the direction of Edmund Randolph, the former Attorney General and Secretary of State under George Washington.

The First Marriage

Tyler soon met and fell in love with Letitia Christian, whose father owned "Cedar Grove." The Christians were influential and the marriage in 1813 strengthened Tyler's social and political connections. His law practice went well and he was elected to the Virginia General Assembly.

He constructed the home *Woodburn* in 1815 and lived there until 1821 when he moved his family to the home of his birth—Greenway. He and Letitia would have eight children but a sad ending when she died during Tyler's presidency after a long illness.

The Right of Nullification

During the nullification crisis, in 1832, South Carolina refused to pay federal tariffs. John Tyler of Virginia, then a Senator, opposed the Force Bill, which gave President

---

Greenway
Birthplace of John Tyler

Still in use, this old Virginia plantation house was the home of Judge John Tyler of Williamsburg. Tyler moved here shortly after his marriage to Mary Armistead in 1776 and lived there until his death. He was a law school roommate and lifelong friend of Thomas Jefferson and served as Speaker of the Virginia House of Delegates. He was a three term governor of Virginia and resigned to accept an appointment as a U. S. District Court judge. Appointed to complete his term as governor was James Monroe. It was at Greenway that the future President John Tyler was born and grew to manhood. His older brother inherited Greenway and sold it to Tyler in 1819. Ten years later, Tyler sold Greenway and moved to Gloucester. It sits off the Old Indian Trail—Route 5—in Charles City County, Virginia about 20 miles west of Williamsburg and is identified by a highway marker near the house. It is privately owned and it is not open to the public.

College of William and Mary

Named for the King and Queen of England who granted the charter in an endowment in 1693, William & Mary is the second oldest institution of higher learning in the United States. The architect was Thomas Hadley, although the plans were those of Christopher Wren, the architect who rebuilt London after the great fire. In 1699, Williamsburg became the Virginia capital and the House of Burgesses met at the college until the Capitol building was constructed. The Wren Building was ready for students in 1700, but it was destroyed by fire in 1705. It was rebuilt on the original foundations, and the chapel was added in 1732. Fire destroyed the northern wing in 1859 and some years later, during the Civil War, other parts of the building were destroyed in the Battle of Williamsburg. The Wren Building was restored by the Colonial Williamsburg Foundation. Three presidents, Thomas Jefferson, James Monroe and John Tyler were educated at William and Mary, as were 16 members of the Continental Congress and four signers of the Declaration of Independence. Phi Beta Kappa was founded there and it was the first college in America to have an honor code for students. It was failing as an institution, with only 22 students, when the Virginia General Assembly debated moving it to the new capital at Richmond. John Tyler, then a member of the House of Delegates championed the historic connection of the school to Williamsburg and convinced the Delegates that it should remain where it was founded.

Visitors: The Sir Christopher Wren Building is open to the public from 10:00 a.m. to 5:00 p.m. weekdays, from 9:00 a.m. to 5:00 p.m. on Saturdays, and from 12:00 noon to 5:00 p.m. on Sundays. The building is closed New Year's Day, Thanksgiving Day and Christmas Day.

Directions: Williamsburg can be reached from I-95, then east on I-64 . The scenic drive is east from Richmond on Route 5 past the James River plantations, including Sherwood Forest and Berkeley. For interactive map http://www.nps.gov/nr/travel/jamesriver/Jamescloseup.htm

Jackson authority to use military force to collect the tariffs. Although Tyler did not approve of South Carolina's willingness to destroy the Union, he acknowledged the constitutional right to do so.

Because the original states had entered into a compact to create the federal government, Tyler believed the states retained the power to withdraw. Tyler's view, expressed in 1833, came to be the interpretation of state sovereignty that led the south out of the Union.

The National Bank

John Tyler was much enamored of Jeffersonian thought and adhered strongly to a view of a limited central government. Elected to the U. S. Senate in 1827, he clashed with Andrew Jackson over a national bank. Although he agreed with Jackson that a national bank was not authorized by the Constitution, he voted to censor the President for trying to drive the bank out of business. Tyler felt that Jackson was acting out of passion rather than reason and that a gradual phasing out of the bank's activities was the proper course.

Later, resolutions were introduced in the Senate to expunge the censor of Jackson. Tyler was instructed by the Virginia General Assembly to support the vote to expunge, but Tyler felt his original decision had been correct. As a

James Semple House

There may have been some type of structure on this lot since 1750. It is believed Thomas Jefferson designed a tripartite house for Dr. William Pasteur in the early 1770s. In a tripartite design, the center section is two stories with the gable on the front elevation, flanked by one story wings. It was purchased about 1799 by Judge James Semple, husband of John Tyler's oldest sister, Anne. Tyler lived here several years while a student at William and Mary. It is sometimes referred to as the Finnie House, for Colonel William Finnie, Quarter-Master General of the Southern Department, who owned the property during the last years of the Revolution. Located in Williamsburg on the south side of Francis Street near the Capitol (between Blair and Walker Streets), the building is privately owned and not open to the public.

point of honor he resigned his senate seat in 1834.

Tyler Becomes a Whig

On the Sunday he was "struck out" of the Senate, Tyler was nominated as Vice President on the Whig ticket. It is difficult to explain why John Tyler accepted the appointment. During his political career, he had disagreed with basic issues which national republicans and anti-Jackson Democrats brought to the Whig party. One of the most important was his belief in states' rights which ruled out his support for a national bank.

Andrew Jackson got his wish that Martin Van Buren succeed him as the country's eighth President. Tyler finished third in the balloting for Vice President and returned to Virginia to devote full time to a law practice in Williamsburg.

After the campaign, it became clear that the Whigs would be dominated by Henry Clay's American System and their program of protective tariffs, internal improvements, and a national bank. Many of Tyler's allies drifted back into the Democratic party. Had Tyler followed them, he would never have become President.

And Tyler Too

One of the candidates for president against Van Buren had been William Henry Harrison who became a favorite of those in the Whig party who opposed Clay. Harrison was thought of as a northern politician, possibly with abolitionist tendencies.

He had made his reputation in Indiana and Ohio, but he was born in Charles City County, Virginia at Berkeley Plantation, also the county of John Tyler's birth. When Harrison won the nomination for president in 1840, the Whigs selected Tyler to run with him to satisfy the strong sentiment in the south for states' rights.

Tyler Becomes President

Following Harrison's election, Tyler returned to his home in Williamsburg. As Vice President, Tyler had no specific duties so there was no reason for him to remain in Washington. When President Harrison died suddenly, only one month after taking office, it put Tyler in the center of a constitutional crisis.

Succession on the death of the president was not clear in the Constitution. The appointees in Harrison's cabinet claimed Tyler was just a vice president "acting as president" and the Cabinet should run the country. Not for a moment however did Tyler doubt that the full power and prestige of the office had vested in him. He resisted all efforts to limit his authority.

John Tyler took the oath of office as president on April 6, 1841 and his term began only two days after Harrison's death.

Tyler's assent to the presidency presented Henry Clay with another opportunity for the presidency. The man who had been rejected as their nominee only months before rallied the Whigs to his banner. Using the national bank as the issue to divide the President from his party, Clay forced two bills for a national bank on Tyler, both of which the President vetoed. When Tyler vetoed the second bank bill, his entire cabinet, except Daniel Webster, resigned. Within six months after assuming the presidency, Tyler was a man without a party.

Severed from his obligations to the Whig party, Tyler was free to move back toward the Democrats and his southern roots. He filled his new cabinet with men who favored the annexation of Texas and opposed abolition and protective tariffs.

Annexation of Texas

Sam Houston had led the Texans to victory at San Jacinto and the Republic of Texas claimed its independence from Mexico. This vast expanse now became a target of the British. With Canada in the north, an alliance with Texas would give England a base in the south and western expansion of the United States would be blocked.

Tyler had burned his bridges to the Whig party and he was not given a second thought when the Whigs nominated Henry Clay for the presidential campaign of 1844. Tyler felt so strongly about Texas becoming a part of the United States that he formed a third party with the slogan "Tyler and Texas."

Tyler's support was strong and the Democrats feared that his candidacy would cut into the vote for their candidate James K. Polk. This started an intensive wooing of Tyler by Democratic leaders. Even Andrew Jackson joined in. Tyler was induced to withdraw his candidacy and throw his support to Polk.

When Polk won the election, it was clear there was strong public support for Texas statehood. Tyler was able to secure the approval of both houses of Congress for annexation just hours before his presidency ended. However, the incoming President Polk would complete the annexation process and receive the lion's share of the credit for bringing Texas into the Union.

Second Marriage

In the third year of his term, Tyler met Julia Gardiner, of New York. Shortly afterward, her father was killed in a tragic accident. Julia's mother was younger than Tyler but she had no objection to his proposal of marriage to her daughter.

With his political life behind him, John Tyler devoted his time to **Sherwood Forest** and raising his children. As the older ones left, new additions took their place. There would be seven more from the second marriage.

Tyler returned to the Democratic party and maintained his interest in the country's affairs. He hoped to rejoin the government in some capacity but no offer ever came.

Life at Sherwood Forest was one of southern gentility and numerous social functions at the great plantations along the James River. He continued to serve on the Board of Visitors at William & Mary, and in the summer there were visits to Villa Marguerite, his home in Hampton, Virginia.

The Peace Conference

The election of Lincoln convinced South Carolina that it must leave the Union. The tension that existed between the industrial north and the slave holding cotton states seemed too great for further discussion after the election. Each of the states had compromised a part of its sovereignty to ratify the Constitution in 1788, but many throughout the south believed that the power of a state to withdraw from the Union had not been surrendered.

John Tyler was among those who believed that the United States was a voluntary federation, and he reacted quickly to form a peace conference to recommend to Congress amendments to the Constitution that would satisfy the concerns of the south.

The commissioners were selected from the border states, along the line that divided the slave from the free states. Tyler believed these states would be the key to finding a solution that would be satisfactory to both north and south.

When the Senate rejected the proposals of the Peace Conference, Tyler returned to Virginia, convinced that it must leave the Union. He felt that if the southern states

The Story of
Sherwood Forest Plantation

John Tyler purchased the plantation Walnut Grove for his wife Letitia Christian. She died while he was president and never visited the new home. After his presidential term was completed, he brought his new bride Julia Gardiner to Walnut Grove. He renamed the plantation Sherwood Forest when his political opponent, Henry Clay, likened him to the legendary English outlaw. The house was increased by sections to 300 feet, and remains the longest frame home in America. The original portion of the home dates from 1730 and was built over an original basement constructed about 1660. A three story wing was connected to the main house in 1780 and additional rooms were added between 1800 and 1830. Tyler added the ballroom for the dancing of the Virginia Reel and a colonnade to connect the main house with the kitchen/laundry. The twenty-five acres of terraced gardens and lawns reflect the style of a plantation home in antebellum Virginia. Sherwood Forest has been the home of the Tyler family since 1842 and the present owners are Mr. and Mrs. Harrison R. Tyler. Harrison Tyler is John Tyler's grandson.

Visitors: There is limited access to Sherwood Forest, for groups and individuals by appointment only. The grounds remain open daily from 9:00 a.m. to 5:00 p.m. for self-guided tours. Please call for more information on house tours. Closed Thanksgiving Day and Christmas Day.

Directions: Sherwood Forest is located 20 miles west of Williamsburg on Virginia Route 5 at 14501 John Tyler Memorial Highway. From Richmond it is 25 miles east on Virginia Route 5.

Contact: Sherwood Forest Plantation, 14501 John Tyler Memorial Highway, Charles City, VA 23030; telephone (804) 829-5377; www.sherwoodforest.org

Sherwood Forest Plantation has been the continuous residence of the Tyler family since the President purchased it in 1842.

143

moved quickly and in unison the north would not use force.

Most of Virginia remained loyal to the Union and would not vote for secession. Then, on April 12, 1861, South Carolina fired on Fort Sumter. President Lincoln responded by asking the states to raise a force of 75,000 men to subdue the rebellion.

Invasion of the south was too much for those who held a higher *loyalty to Virginia*. The day after Lincoln's announcement, the state which had contributed more than any other in leadership and resources to break away from England and form the United States now voted to leave it.

Loyalty to Virginia

Slavery was the spark that blew the Union apart, but it was the sovereignty of the states that was decided on the battlefields of the Civil War. The states had existed, in the case of Virginia, for two hundred years before they agreed to be united by the Constitution. Especially in the agrarian south, history and family connected them to the land and tradition. Loyalty to their native states was the unifying force of the new Confederacy. The former U. S. President, John Tyler was the principal organizer of the "Peace Conference." When that failed, he was elected as a delegate to the new Confederate Congress. Many graduates of West Point became officers in the Confederate Army, of whom the most noted were Virginia's Robert E. Lee and Thomas J. "Stonewall" Jackson. The ambassador for the Confederacy to England was James Mason, the grandson of George Mason, author of Virginia's Declaration of Rights. The Secretary of War of the Confederacy was George Randolph, grandson of Thomas Jefferson. When Robert E. Lee surrendered at Appomattox, one of his aides was Lieutenant Colonel Charles Marshall, the grandson of John Marshall, a colonel in the Continental Army during the Revolutionary war who became Chief Justice of the United States Supreme Court. Richard Taylor, son of former President Zachary Taylor, commanded a brigade under Stonewall Jackson. President Taylor's daughter, Sarah Knox Taylor was the first wife of Jefferson Davis. John Augustine Washington III, the last owner of Mount Vernon, was killed in a skirmish while a member of Robert E. Lee's staff.

Last Days

In July, 1861, Tyler cheered the southern victory in the opening battle of the war at Manassas Virginia. He was the overwhelming choice to represent Charles City County in the new Confederate Congress. Several months later, before his term began, Tyler became ill and several days later quietly passed away.

His last words were, "Doctor, I am going." The long funeral cortege took him from St. Paul's church to Richmond to Hollywood Cemetery. The war John Tyler had struggled to prevent rolled across the South and his concept of Virginia's sovereignty was swept away.

The United States on the eve of the Civil War

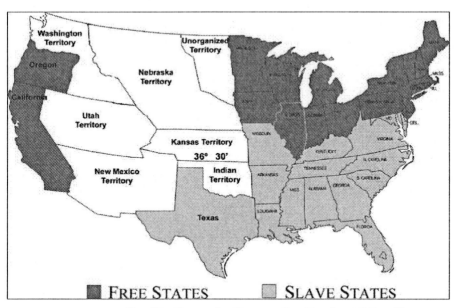

Credit: Catoctin Center for Regional Studies

ZACHARY TAYLOR
The Twelfth President

Birthplace: Barboursville

Date of Birth: November 24, 1784

Term: March 5, 1849 – July 9, 1850

Vice President: Millard Fillmore

1849 –1850

Date of Death: July 9, 1850

Burial Place: Zachary Taylor National Cemetery, Louisville, Kentucky

His career as a soldier was the story of America's expansion westward.

Early Years

After the Revolutionary War, Richard Taylor returned to Orange County, Virginia and in 1779 he married Sarah Dabney Strother. Like many of the Revolutionary War veterans the Continental Congress could not pay, Richard Taylor was awarded land in Kentucky as a bonus. He decided to sell his property, Hare Forest, in Orange County, Virginia, which was not productive, and move his family to Kentucky.

At the time, his wife was well into her pregnancy and remained behind at **Montebello**, the home of Taylor's cousin. It is likely this was the birthplace of Zachary Taylor, the third of their ten children, on November 24, 1784.

A year later, Richard Taylor returned and brought Zachary and his mother to Springfield, to a log cabin on Beargrass Creek east of Louisville. Richard Taylor became a substantial landowner and held a number of civil positions, including presidential elector for James Madison and James Monroe.

Montebello
Birthplace of Zachary Taylor

Zachary Taylor was born in Orange County, Virginia but his exact place of birth remains a subject of debate. Zachary's father, Richard, left his home Hare Forest in Orange County to claim a land grant in Kentucky as payment for his revolutionary war service. Hare Forest is privately owned and is not open to the public. Richard's wife could not travel because of her advanced pregnancy and Zachary Taylor was most likely born at Montebello, a plantation home of Richard Taylor's cousin, situated between Barboursville and Gordonsville. Montebello is privately owned and is not open to the public. There is a highway marker located on Virginia Route 33 below Montebello which states:

Montebello

Here was born Zachary Taylor, twelfth

president of the United States. November 12,

1784. Taylor commanding an American army,

won the notable Battle of Buena Vista

in Mexico 1847.

James Taylor II was the great grandfather of both Zachary Taylor and James Madison. James Taylor II built Bloomsbury, now the oldest home in Orange County. Bloomsbury is now a private museum and appointments to visit may be requested of Helen Marie Taylor at (540) 672-2875. James Taylor II gave Meadow Farm to Zachary Taylor, Sr., grandfather of the president, Zachary Taylor. It is privately owned and is not open to the public. James Taylor II also gave the land to his son-in-law, Ambrose Madison, grandfather of the president James Madison, on which Montpelier was built. Many of the homes in Orange County remain associated with both the Taylor and Madison families. They are sometimes opened to the public during house tours. Contact the Orange County Department of Tourism and Visitor's Bureau, (877) 222-8072.

A Soldier's Life

Although Louisville was the frontier during Zachary Taylor's youth, by the time he accepted a commission in the army in 1808, it had become a thriving city. Taylor had little formal schooling and how he got his commission is unclear although he was competent enough in mathematics to perform surveying.

Several years later, the young lieutenant married Margaret Mackall Smith. She accepted the hardship of army life on frontier posts and raised three children to adulthood.

After the United States declared war on England in June 1812, the English encouraged the Indians to attack American settlements on the western frontier. Taylor was ordered to Fort Harrison, a post north of Vincennes, Indiana.

When the Indians attacked, Taylor's cool handling of the defense of the fort was noticed by William Henry Harrison, Commander of the Northwest Territory. Taylor was breveted a major for his gallantry.

Life on the Frontier

After the war, there was a severe reduction in the size of the army and Taylor was unhappy to be reduced to his former rank of captain. He left the Army and engaged in land speculation. Taylor's situation was known to President Madison and within four years Taylor was back in uniform with his promotion.

He was also acquainted with President Monroe and by 1819, Zachary Taylor was a lieutenant colonel. For the next dozen years, Taylor served at various posts along the Mississippi from Louisiana to Green Bay in countless skirmishes as the Indians resisted the pressure from America's westward flow.

White settlers were also crowding out the Seminoles in Florida but the Indians refused to move west to the reservations set aside by the government. Zachary Taylor spent two years in Florida fighting the Seminoles. He earned his general's star and gained the nickname "Old Rough and Ready," for his willingness to live on the field and suffer the same deprivations as his soldiers.

His military skills, so long in the making, marked him as an outstanding field commander. His next assignment to the Texas frontier would vault him into national prominence and eventually the presidency.

War in Mexico

Americans began moving into the Mexican territory of Texas in the 1820's. Mexico banned further immigration in 1830 and the Texans revolted. They won independence at the Battle of San Jacinto and formed the Republic of Texas in 1836. Great Britain, still seeking a way to stop America's westward movement, tried to establish an alliance with Texas.

Texas had slaves and the nation divided north and south on whether slavery should continue if it became part of the United States. President John Tyler believed Texas should join the Union and he was successful in obtaining a joint resolution of Congress on February 28, 1845, just before his term expired, annexing the Republic of Texas.

General Taylor moved his troops to Corpus Christi in the event Mexico tried to prevent the Texas Congress from accepting the annexation treaty. Taylor was ordered to hold the Rio Grande River as the border between Texas and Mexico.

When the Mexican commander Arista took his army across the river, on April 24, 1846, Congress declared war. Taylor intercepted the Mexicans at Palo Alto. After a fierce engagement, Arista withdrew. The next day Taylor launched an attack at Resaca de la Palma. This time, the Mexicans broke and fled back over the Rio Grande.

"Old Rough and Ready" continued the pursuit into Mexico and ran into a large army under Santa Anna. Outnumbered three to one, Taylor fell back to Buena Vista. The Mexicans launched attacks on Taylor's defenses for two days, but all were broken by the fire of the American guns. At one of the decisive points on the battlefield stood the Mississippians, led by Taylor's former son-in-law, Jefferson

Davis.

Santa Anna marched away to Mexico City leaving General Taylor in control of northern Mexico. When the great fortress of Chapultepec in Mexico City — the Halls of Montezuma — fell before the Americans, Mexico asked for peace. The Treaty of Guadalupe Hidalgo, in February 1848, ended the war.

Mexico ceded New Mexico and California and agreed that the Rio Grande would be the southern border of Texas. The United States now stretched from ocean to ocean and Zachary Taylor returned to the United States a war hero. A town in Virginia established 1899, was likely named after the Battle of Buena Vista, but a direct connection has not been found.

Whigs Capture Taylor

President Polk had guided the nation through the Mexican War, but did not want a second term. The Democrats split into two factions, largely over the issue of slavery. Many who opposed the spread of slavery to any new states admitted to the Union flooded into the Whig party. William Henry Harrison, the first Whig president, also had won national attention as a general. Now the Whigs courted the popular Zachary Taylor.

The anniversary of the Battle of Buena Vista coincided with the celebration of George Washington's birthday and increased the interest in a soldier president. Taylor continued to say that others were more qualified and that he did not want to be a candidate. He did feel that the Whigs were closer to the ideals of the limited government of Thomas Jefferson. He remained at his post as Commander of the Western District and refused to campaign but his supporters continued without him and secured his nomination at the Whig convention.

Although Taylor did not have a well formed political philosophy, he did agree that slavery should not be expanded into the new territory acquired from Mexico. Taylor had slaves at his Cypress Grove plantation, but he opposed the extension of slavery.

He viewed the president as supreme in foreign affairs, but conceded that Congress had primary responsibility for the domestic area. In the presidential election, Zachary Taylor did not carry his native state, Virginia. Out of thirty states, he won the popular vote in fifteen, and won a decisive majority in the electoral college.

Taylor had risen to the nation's highest office on the reputation he earned as a soldier in the Mexican War. His success in that conflict helped bring to the U. S. a vast territory. His first issue as president was the future of the expanded country. Whether it would be divided into slave states or free states brought the nation once again to the brink of disunion.

Glimpse of Disunion

After the Treaty of Guadalupe-Hidalgo ended the war, military governments were set up in the areas acquired from Mexico. Anti-slavery forces of the northeast wanted slavery banned from all the new territories. The slave states threatened secession unless the option for slavery was left open. Taylor responded in his inaugural address that he would uphold the "integrity" of the Union.

Taylor was in favor of California and New Mexico bypassing territorial status and coming in as free states. His views had little impact on the Congress, the first in which the president's party did not have a majority in either house. The conflict between the abolitionists and the slave states would be temporarily solved by the *Compromise of 1850.*

Last Days

Zachary Taylor did not live to see the "Compromise." He died on July 9, 1850, some sixteen months after taking office. His last illness apparently resulted from drinking ice and eating cherries after spending the Fourth of July in the hot sun. He developed severe intestinal discomfort the next day and he grew gradually weaker. One of his last comments was to his doctors, "You have fought a good fight, but you cannot make a stand."

Compromise of 1850

Out of the vast area acquired from Mexico under the Treaty of Guadalupe-Hidalgo would come the states of California and New Mexico, most of Arizona, Nevada and Utah and a part of Colorado. However, the Missouri Compromise of 1820 provided that all new states, except Missouri, above the latitude line of 36° 30' N would be free. It was clear that a division of the territory by this line would result in a greater number of free states. Some slave states openly threatened secession if the balance of power shifted. Under a compromise, led by Henry Clay and Daniel Webster, California would be a free state. In the remaining territory, the inhabitants of the new states would decide in their constitutions whether to permit slavery, a doctrine known as "popular sovereignty." The main concession to the slave states was the Fugitive Slave Law. Slaves who fled to free states were not free and had to be returned. Finally, the slave trade, but not slavery, was banned in the nation's capitol. These measures were a series of acts by Congress, but they came to be grouped as the Compromise of 1850.

Because of the sudden onset of his illness, *rumors of poisoning* Taylor for his rejection of the slave states persisted, until exhumation in 1991 finally ended this suspicion.

At the time of Taylor's death, thirty states had been admitted to the union. Two months later, the state of California was admitted, occupying 60% of the Pacific coast line. There were some gaps in the interior which would eventually be filled, but for all practical purposes, America now stretched from sea to shining sea.

Taylor's body was transported to Louisville, Kentucky where he was buried. A short decade later the Union he had helped to expand broke apart. The dead from the conflict he worked to avoid during his short stay in office would be buried around him. The cemetery was later named the Zachary Taylor National Cemetery.

Rumors of Poisoning

When Zachary Taylor fell ill and suddenly died, there were suspicions that he had been murdered. His opposition to the extension of slavery drew a bitter reaction. The official cause of death was gastroenteritis, the inflammation of the stomach and intestines, but the rumor had persisted that he was poisoned. In 1991, Taylor's descendants agreed that his remains could be exhumed from the Zachary Taylor National Cemetery in Louisville, Kentucky and examined at the Oak Ridge National Laboratory. If he had been poisoned, the likely agent was arsenic, which is present in most human bodies. However, the test revealed that the arsenic levels in Taylor's body were several hundred times less than what would have been necessary to cause his death. Those who had been under suspicion for so many years finally had been cleared.

The flag of the United States representing the 34 states in the Union at the time that the Confederate States fired on Fort Sumter in 1861. Although stars were added for states that joined during the Civil War, the stars for the states of the Confederacy were never removed.

WOODROW WILSON

The Twenty-Eighth President

Birthplace: Staunton

Date of Birth: December 28, 1856

Term: March 4, 1913-March 3, 1921

Vice President: Thomas Riley Marshall

1913-1921

Date of Death: February 3, 1924

Burial Place: Washington Cathedral

*His great vision was an ordered world
through a League of Nations.*

Early Years

Joseph Ruggles Wilson studied at Princeton Theological Seminary at the College of New Jersey. He became a Presbyterian minister and married Janet "Jessie" Woodrow, the daughter of a Presbyterian minister. He began his pastorate at the First Presbyterian Church in Staunton, Virginia.

Twenty-one months later, on December 28, 1856, Thomas Woodrow Wilson, the third of four children was born. The Presbyterian manse was ***Wilson's birthplace home.*** Several years later, Wilson's father became pastor of a church in Augusta, Georgia, where he helped found the Southern Presbyterian Church.

"Tommie" Wilson spent his boyhood watching the tragedy and aftermath of the civil war unfold. He did not learn to read until he was twelve but was able to enter Davidson College in North Carolina when he was seventeen. After one year, he left because of ill health. It was more than

Wilson' Birthplace Home
The Woodrow Wilson Presidential Library
and Museum

The Reverend Joseph Ruggles Wilson became pastor of the Staunton Presbyterian Church in December 1854. Several months later, he moved his wife and two daughters into the Presbyterian Manse. Thomas Woodrow Wilson was born there in 1856 on the eve of the Civil War. It remained a Presbyterian Manse until it was acquired by the Trustees of Mary Baldwin College. The College held the house as a memorial to the President and in 1930 transferred it to the Woodrow Wilson Birthplace Foundation, Inc. After restoration was completed in 1941, it was opened to the public. There is also a presidential museum and a research library. Wilson returned to his birthplace during his youth and again when he celebrated his 56th birthday, several months before he assumed the presidency.

Visitors: There are guided tours of the birthplace home, but self-guided tours are permitted for the museum. Both are open daily from 9:00 a.m. to 5:00 p.m. and Sundays from 12:00 Noon to 5:00 p.m. Closed Tuesday and Wednesday in January and February. Call for group tours. Closed Thanksgiving, Christmas Eve, Christmas Day, New Year's Day and Easter. There is a museum shop with collectibles and books.

Directions: From I-81, take U. S. Route 25 west to downtown Staunton. Follow signage to the house.

Contact: Woodrow Wilson Birthplace Foundation, 20 North Coalter Street, Staunton, Virginia 24401; (540)885-0897; www.woodrowwilson.org

The home In Staunton, Virginia in which Woodrow Wilson was born is now a museum and presidential library

a year before he returned to school, but this time he enrolled in Princeton. He was a good but not an exemplary student.

After graduation in 1879, he attended the University of Virginia Law School but left during his second year because of a stomach disorder. Severe headaches as well as stomach problems would plague him the rest of his life.

Wilson was admitted to practice law in Georgia and opened an office in Atlanta. When he was unable to attract any clients, he became disenchanted with the routine of a lawyer and decided his future was in education. He enrolled in a doctoral program at Johns Hopkins University in Baltimore to become a teacher.

While at Hopkins, Wilson wrote *Congressional Government*, where he raised the idea that issues should be debated in public. He felt it was the function of the president, and not Congress, who should identify the needs of the people.

Educator

By 1885, he was no longer "Tommie," but Woodrow Wilson. That year, he married Ellen Louise Axson, the daughter of a preacher, in the Independent Presbyterian Church in Savannah, Georgia. She became a companion and confidant and his mentor in the appreciation of literature and the beauty of nature. Over the next four years they had three daughters, Margaret Wilson, Jessie Woodrow Wilson and Eleanor Randolph Wilson.

At the time of his marriage, Wilson began his teaching career at Bryn Mawr, a small women's college in Middletown, Connecticut. He was not happy teaching women and several years later accepted an offer as professor of history at Wesleyan University.

In 1889, he published his book on comparative government, *The State*. Wilson felt the national government should monitor economy and business. It should serve a broad public interest and oversee a distribution of the wealth. This received wide acclaim and led to an invitation by Princeton for Wilson to become a professor of jurisprudence and political economy.

His reputation grew at Princeton, and in 1902, he accepted the offer to become its president. Perhaps influenced by the Jefferson design at the University of Virginia, Wilson tried to redesign Princeton by grouping the colleges around a central court with dormitories and cafeterias for all the students. This was a democratic ideal because it placed all the students on an equal footing, but the alumni opposed the plan because it would eliminate the 'eating clubs' that had rules of admission.

To the alumni he sounded his later political legacy. "The great voice of America...comes in a murmur from the hills and woods and farms and factories and mills...from the homes of common men."

When his reforms were rejected, Wilson resigned. He felt he was right and his personality made it difficult for him to compromise. In 1908, he published *Constitutional Government in the United States.* His political views and the controversy at Princeton caught the eye of New Jersey's politicians and Wilson was urged to run for governor in 1910.

Wilson Becomes President

The public had a favorable opinion of Wilson's efforts to erase the social divisions at Princeton. Although New Jersey was run by machine politics, Wilson received their support. He never promised them anything in return. After he won, he ignored the political bosses and instituted reforms for schools, elections, and public utilities.

Wilson clearly had his eye on the presidency and he used the attention his state reform movement attracted to introduce himself to the nation. The Democratic convention in 1912 went to 46 ballots before Wilson won the nomination. Wilson stressed in his campaign that the operation of government was too much influenced by special interests. He wanted it to operate for the benefit of the people and he attracted progressives from both parties. Wilson was aided greatly when the former president, Theodore Roosevelt, formed a third party (Bull Moose). This split the Republican vote and made Wilson an overwhelming winner in the Electoral College.

America had voted for reform and Wilson did not waste time putting his ideas to the test. His first term saw the adoption of a central banking system and creation of the Federal Reserve Board, a commission for unfair trade practices, limits on child labor, removal of tariffs on import and high taxes for the wealthy. In spite of the progressive movement Wilson brought to the presidency, he never became an advocate for *civil rights.*

Crisis in Mexico

Immediately after the election, a revolution in Mexico installed a dictatorship. President Wilson called for Mexico to return its constitutional leaders to power. There was no basis for American intervention until several American sailors were arrested while on shore leave in Mexico. Shortly afterward, a German ship was discovered delivering arms to the rebels. Based on a claim of foreign intervention in violation of the Monroe Doctrine, Wilson sent the Marines into Vera Cruz.

Civil Rights

Woodrow Wilson viewed women in a manner traditional for one of his time. He was unhappy in his first teaching position at Bryn Mawr and welcomed the change to move to Wesleyan where he "could teach men." The Democratic party platform in 1916 endorsed women's suffrage but it took a campaign of picketing and demonstrations before Wilson gave it his active support. Wilson followed rather than led in the adoption of the Nineteenth Amendment giving women the right to vote. His southern heritage may also have affected his attitude toward blacks. There was no interest in the administration to end segregation in government or defense industries. Although 350,000 African-Americans served in World War I, the military continued in a segregated manner. After the war, race riots erupted in St. Louis and Chicago which required federal intervention. Wilson condemned the morality of these conditions but never pursued a program for racial equality.

Upset with Wilson's interference in Mexico's internal affairs, rebels led by Pancho Villa raided New Mexico. An American force crossed into Mexico in March, 1916, and chased Villa for a year. Wilson believed his actions were necessary to preserve constitutional government in Mexico.

American troops also went into Haiti, Nicaragua and the Dominican Republic. Wilson intervened, not only for American interests, but to help these countries. It was Wilson's hope to form a Pan-American alliance that would respect boundaries and settle disputes without war.

The Great War

While America dealt with these small conflicts in its own hemisphere, the winds of war blew over Europe. When Serbian nationalists assassinated Archduke Ferdinand, heir to the Austro–Hungarian throne, Austria-Hungary declared war on Serbia. A pre-existing treaty brought Russia to the aid of Serbia, and Germany came to the support of Austria. France saw an opportunity to recover the provinces of Alsace and Lorraine, and entered the war against Germany. Although Kaiser Wilhelm II, the Emperor of Germany, was cousin to both George V, King of England, and Alexandra, Empress of Russia, a treaty with France pulled England into the conflict on the side of France and Russia.

There was a strong isolationist feeling in the United States that this war was a European affair and America should not be involved. Wilson had just suffered the loss of his wife Ellen and for a while it greatly affected his ability to deal with the war.

England used its naval superiority to blockade the shipping lanes. In retaliation, Germany launched submarine warfare against all merchant ships. Wilson warned Germany not to attack America's neutral ships, but on May 7, 1915, a German submarine sank the Lusitania with the loss of 128 Americans. Under the threat that the United States would break off all diplomatic relations, Germany backed down and promised its submarines would not attack unarmed merchant ships.

Woodrow Wilson tried to bring the warring countries

to the peace table. He proposed that the combatants return to their position before the war—a "peace without victory."

England thought it would win the war and wanted terms to make certain Germany would not wage war in the future. It proposed a "League of Nations" to keep peace after the war. Germany answered with a declaration of unrestricted submarine warfare. All ships which entered a zone around Great Britain, France and Italy would be sunk.

Fourteen Points

England continued its public relation campaign to sway the American people to enter the war against Germany. Americans did not understand the purpose of the war and Wilson maintained a neutral course. The war became a major issue in Wilson's campaign for a second term. Republicans criticized Wilson's attitude toward Germany as cowardly, but it made the Republican campaign sound like a war party.

Voters in favor of continued neutrality and peace moved to Wilson under the slogan, "He kept us out of war." Progressives supported Wilson for his reform legislation. Advocating peace, prosperity and progress, Wilson took a solid south and all but two states west of the Mississippi.

Within a month of his reelection, the President could not longer ignore the continued German attacks on American ships. Appearing before the Congress, he declared that war had been "thrust upon" the United States. Wilson put the war in moral terms. Declaring that "the world must be made safe for democracy," Wilson asked Congress for a declaration of war on April 2, 1917.

Wilson believed that the American people would not fight for "a selfish aim," so he listed the goals of the war in fourteen points. These included freedom of the seas, reduction of armaments, adjustment of colonial claims, withdrawal of Germany from Russia, Belgium and France, and autonomy for Austria, Hungary and Poland. Point 14 provided for an "association of nations," which would guarantee to all states "independence and territorial integrity."

By the time U. S. troops arrived in France, in 1918, more than 1.5 million soldiers, English and French, had died over the three years of the war. Opposing trench lines stretched five hundred miles from the North Sea to the Swiss border.

The Americans went into the line in June, just as the Germans began major offensives to break the stalemate. By September, over a million Americans were in the Meuse-Argonne offensive. For forty-seven days the push continued as the German lines broke and retreated. Germany sought an armistice based on Wilson's Fourteen Points.

League of Nations

When President Wilson arrived in France, he did not review the American troops, but hurried to the Peace Conference in Paris. The armistice was signed on November 11, 1918 and Wilson went on a victory tour of Europe. Everywhere, the crowds cheered for him and for the Americans who had come to save the world for democracy. Wilson also came with a bold proposal of a world order. It would be called the League of Nations through which the member states would yield power to a common good.

When the treaty ending the war was signed in the great palace at Versailles, most of the Fourteen Points disappeared. In the end, the Treaty of Versailles met the demands of England and France, which included the loss of German territories and payment of reparations. The Peace Conference redrew the borders of Europe and created new countries. Wilson remained confident the League of Nations would correct any injustices in the Treaty.

However, the endless days of sorting out the new boundaries of Europe and assigning the spoils of war had slowly drained the President's strength. He became gaunt and nervous. His once self assured and jaunty personality became dour and suspicious.

Wilson came home from Europe exhausted and on the edge of a complete breakdown. He also returned to rising opposition as American public opinion favored the separation from Europe established by the Monroe Doctrine.

The Rejected Prophet

One of the objections in the United States Congress to the League of Nations was the surrender of American sovereignty to a world government. Wilson felt there was sufficient protection for the United States and refused to discuss further changes to the Covenant of the League of Nations. He dismissed the politicians who opposed him and placed his faith in the American people to recognize he was right.

Wilson began a nationwide campaign in July, 1919, to rally public support for the League of Nations. As the tour progressed, the crowds became larger and more enthusiastic. His doctor had warned him not to undertake this cross-country tour. Inevitably, the burden of daily travel and speeches proved too great. Completely used up, Wilson collapsed.

A stroke paralyzed his left side and affected his speech. His ability to reason was impaired which magnified character traits of self-righteousness and stubbornness. His refusal to compromise the concerns of Congress to the Covenant led to its defeat.

It was brought up for a second vote and still Wilson refused any changes. He allowed a margin of seven votes to defeat his great dream. The country Europe looked to as essential to the League of Nations would not be a member.

Shadow President

Edith Bolling Galt had been introduced to Woodrow Wilson by his daughters. He was immediately captivated. Wilson needed to replace the love he had with his first wife. A little more than a year after Ellen's death, he had married Edith. She did not have a college education and no previous connection with political Washington.

After his stroke, Wilson could not fully perform the duties of the presidency. Edith Wilson watched her husband's almost helpless physical condition and his diminished mental capacity. To save his life, she sealed him off. Only his doctor was permitted to see him. She took messages to him and delivered his answers and was accused of trying to act as a "shadow president."

Because of her efforts to shield him from the pressures of the presidency the government lurched along leaderless. The cabinet secretaries continued to run their departments without direction from the White House. No one was more concerned than the vice-president, Thomas Marshall. Wilson had never confided in him, and now, with the country leaderless, there was no constitutional procedure to pass to him the reins of power.

Wilson slowly regained his mental abilities and could participate in meetings. He remained weak however, and rarely appeared in public. He saw the coming presidential election in 1920 as a chance for the American people to rise to the support of the League of Nations. It was not to be.

Wilson sought the nomination, but the Democratic Party selected James Cox and Franklin Roosevelt. The Republican candidate, Warren Harding, promised in his campaign there would be no entanglement of the United States in the League of Nations. He won a resounding victory. Even after this rejection by the American voters, Woodrow Wilson was confident that in the future his vision would come to pass.

Last Years

In March, 1921, Wilson left the White House. He moved to **the house on S Street** purchased for Wilson by a group of his friends. An old friend set up a law practice for him, but he only visited the office one time. A little over a year later, the firm folded, a victim to Wilson's constant ethical objections to prospective clients.

Although too weak to participate in the ceremony, Wilson attended the dedication of the Tomb of the Unknown Soldier at Arlington Cemetery on Armistice Day, November 1921.

Wilson suffered from the deaths of the Americans he sent to die in France. In the car rides about the countryside after his presidency, whenever he would spot soldiers on the road, he would always acknowledge them with a salute.

In some cases, he would have the car stopped and speak directly to the men.

He tried to write. He had been taught the delight of words by his preacher father. Words had carried him to the pinnacle of power. Now, words failed him.

Wilson looked forward to the presidential campaign in 1924. Although his strength had not returned, he wanted to run again. He had signed the Treaty of Versailles, but the Senate, invoking the Monroe Doctrine, turned away from Wilson and rejected the treaty. The Democratic Party paid little attention to Wilson's interest in the presidency..

Wilson had staked his political reputation and his health on the League of Nations and a new international order. He felt it was a "gross and criminal blunder" that the United States rejected the Treaty of Versailles and membership in the League of Nations. His hope was that the League of Nations would rectify the inequities that had been written into the Treaty.

None of these plans were to be realized, as his weakened body slipped into its final illness. His last sentence was, "I am ready." He died two days later, on February 3, 1924. He was buried in the National Cathedral in Washington, D.C. where a stained glass window above his sarcophagus depicts events of his life. He is the only president buried in Washington DC.

House on S Street
The President Woodrow Wilson House

Selected by Edith Wilson, the house was at the edge of Washington, D.C. It was a Georgian design with a formal entrance, five bedrooms and a small garden in the rear. It was built about four years before she purchased it in 1921. Wilson added an electric elevator and garage. An adjacent unimproved lot was also purchased for privacy. Wilson moved into the house following the completion of his second term as president and lived there until his death on February 3, 1924. The house was left to the National Trust for Historic Preservation as a gift from Wilson's wife to perpetuate the Legacy of Woodrow Wilson. It has been operated as a museum since 1963 and is devoted to Wilson's Washington's years (1912-1924), and displays articles from the Wilson presidency as well as family and personal items. The house has been organized as a "living textbook" of what American life was like in the 1920's.

Visitors: The Museum is open Tuesday through Sunday from 10:00 a.m. to 4:00 p.m. and is closed on Mondays and major holidays. Tours are guided. Please call for groups of more than ten, and for information on handicap accessibility.

Directions: The President Woodrow Wilson House is located just off Embassy Row, Massachusetts Avenue, at 24th Street. Nearest Metro stop: Dupont Circle on the Red Line. Take the Q Street exit, travel north on Massachusetts Avenue five blocks to 24th Street, turn right and then a right on S Street.

Contact: Woodrow Wilson House, 2340 S Street, N.W., Washington, DC, 20008; (202) 387-4062; www.woodrowwilsonhouse.org

The only presidential museum in Washington, D.C., The President Woodrow Wilson House returns the visitor to the 1920s.

Appendix 1

The Vice Presidents

George Washington

JOHN ADAMS was vice president during both of Washington's terms, 1789-1797. He was born in Braintree (now Quincy), Massachusetts on October 19, 1735. He attended Harvard College and after graduation in 1751 studied under a local attorney until his admission to the bar.

Several years later, Adams heard James Otis argue against the Writs of Assistance imposed by the British. This greatly influenced him in his response to the Stamp Act, which he found "inconsistent with the spirit of the common law and of the essential fundamental principles of the British constitution." He later argued, in his defense of John Hancock for customs duty violations, that the British could not tax the colonies without their consent.

He served as counsel for the British soldiers who fired on the crowd in the "Boston Massacre" of 1770, but this did not prevent him from being elected to the Massachusetts Assembly.

As a member of the Continental Congress, he was appointed to a committee to prepare the Declaration of Independence and urged Thomas Jefferson to prepare the draft.

Following the war, he wrote the Massachusetts constitution which provided for three branches of government, executive, legislative and judicial. However, Adams was a believer in a strong central government. When he ran for president following Washington's voluntary withdrawal after two terms, opposition from the "republicans" led by Jefferson began to form. When he ran for a second term in 1800, he was defeated by Jefferson.

He died at Quincy, Massachusetts on July 4, 1826, and is buried at the United First Parish Church in Quincy, Massachusetts.

Thomas Jefferson

AARON BURR was vice president during Jefferson's first term, 1801-1805. He was born in Newark, New Jersey, on February 6, 1756. Burr attended the College of New Jersey (now Princeton University) and was a hero of the Battle of Saratoga, an early and important victory in the Revolutionary War.

After the war, he became a successful lawyer in New York and in the presidential election of 1800, he tied with Jefferson in electoral votes. The procedure at that time sent the election to the House of Representatives which decided for Jefferson. The Twelfth Amendment to the Constitution was later passed to avoid this type of dead-lock in presidential elections.

While still vice president, Burr ran for governor of New York. Alexander Hamilton campaigned against him and because of Hamilton's comments Burr challenged him to a duel. Burr killed Hamilton and was indicted for murder in New Jersey and New York but was never tried. He finished out his term as vice president but Jefferson dropped him from the ticket for a second term.

Several years later, Jefferson had him charged with conspiracy for a plot to take over western territory to gain control of the gateway to the Mississippi at New Orleans. Burr was acquitted and left the United States, but eventually returned to marry a wealthy widow. He died on September 14, 1836 and was buried in Princeton Cemetery, Princeton, N. J.

GEORGE CLINTON was vice president from 1805-1809, during Jefferson's second term. Clinton was born on July 26, 1739 in Little Britain, Orange County, N. Y. He was a delegate to the Second Continental Congress and served as a brigadier general of militia in the Revolution and for twenty-one years as governor of New York.

He initially opposed ratification of the U. S. Constitution because he opposed the states relinquishing power to the central government. He was the first vice president elected as a "running mate" under the Twelfth Amendment.

James Madison

GEORGE CLINTON was vice president from 1809-1812 during Madison's first term. He unsuccessfully sought the presidential nomination in 1808, but then agreed to serve as Madison's vice president although he held a low opinion of Madison.

He was the first man to serve as vice president under two different presidents. He died before completing his second term on April 20, 1812 and is buried in the First Dutch Reformed Church Cemetery, in Kingston, N. Y.

ELBRIDGE GERRY was vice president during Madison's second term from 1813-1814. He was born on July 17, 1744 in Marble Head, Massachusetts. Gerry graduated from Harvard College and worked in the family mercantile business until he became involved in the opposition to England's tax on tea.

He served in the Continental Congress from 1776 to 1786, and was a signer of the Declaration of Independence. He was also a signer of the Articles of Confederation as well as a member of the 1787 Constitutional Convention.

The word "gerrymandering" ("Gerry" plus "salamander") was first used to describe an oddly shaped congressional district approved by Gerry when he was governor of Massachusetts to benefit the Democratic- Republican Party. It now means any political district drawn to favor a political party.

Although he first opposed the Constitution because of a concern that too much power was given to a central government, he later came to support it and was elected to serve in Congress. Gerry supported Madison in the War of 1812 against Federalist attacks.

Madison picked him as vice president to help with the campaign in the northeast. He died unexpectedly after approximately 18 months in office on November 23, 1814 in

Washington, D.C. and is buried in Congressional Cemetery, Washington, D.C.

James Monroe

DANIEL D. TOMPKINS was vice president during both of Monroe's terms, 1817-1825. He was born on June 21, 1774 in Fox Meadow (now Scarsdale), New York. Tompkins graduated first in his class from Columbia College in New York City, and practiced law there. He entered into a successful political career and eventually gained an appointment as an associate justice of the New York Supreme Court.

He was elected governor of New York in 1807 and was a strong supporter of Madison in the War of 1812 and used not only his own funds but personally guaranteed loans to finance the state militia. He was unsuccessful in his bid for the presidential nomination in 1816, but agreed to accept the vice presidency under Monroe.

A wartime borrowing scandal haunted Tompkins throughout his term of office when muddled record keeping led to charges he had taken state funds. He was eventually vindicated, but by then he was plagued by a severe drinking problem and broken health.

He died at age 50 on June 11, 1825, in Staten Island, New York, shortly after his term as vice president was completed, the shortest lived of all the vice presidents. He is buried in the Minthorne Vault, St. Mark's Church in-the-Bowery, New York City.

William Henry Harrison

JOHN TYLER was vice president for only one month in Harrison's first term. Tyler was born March 29, 1790 in Charles City County, Virginia. He was a rigid believer in Jeffersonian democracy, but broke with the democrats over President Andrew Jackson's handling of the national bank issue.

He agreed to serve as vice president on the Whig ticket with Harrison who died within a month of the election. The Constitution was unclear on the role the vice president was to play, but Tyler took the position that he was not an "acting president," nor was he a vice president "substituting" for the president, but had in fact become the president upon Harrison's death. It was his forceful insistence that set the precedent for future vice presidents.

John Tyler

The Constitution did not provide for a method to replace the vice president when the president died, so Tyler served until the end of his term in 1845 without a vice president. That situation was not resolved until the 1967 adoption of the Twenty-fifth Amendment to the Constitution.

Zachary Taylor

MILLARD FILLMORE was vice president in Taylor's first term, 1849-1850. He was born on January 7, 1800 in the frontier town of Locke (now Summerhill), Cayuga County, New York. He was never formally educated and was largely self taught. He was able to work as a teacher and later as a law clerk and gained admission to the New York bar in 1824.

Fillmore became a Whig and supported Henry Clay's American system of internal improvements, tariffs and national bank, all of which brought him into opposition as a member of the House of Representatives with the administration of John Tyler. He also opposed the Texas annexation in his losing bid for governor of New York in 1844.

Fillmore became Taylor's vice presidential candidate to heal the schism in the party that occurred when Taylor defeated Henry Clay for the presidential nomination. When Taylor died in 1850, after only 18 months in office, Fillmore became president.

As president, he later signed the fugitive slave law, which split the Whig party and denied him the nomination to run for president in the next election. He returned to politics in 1856 as the nominee of the American party, anti-Catholic, anti-immigrant and nicknamed the "Know-Nothings."

He suffered an overwhelming defeat, carrying only one state, Maryland. He returned to New York and served as the first chancellor of the University of Buffalo and the first president of the Buffalo Historical Society. He died on March 8, 1874 in Buffalo, New York and is buried in Forest Lawn Cemetery, Buffalo, New York.

Woodrow Wilson

THOMAS RILEY MARSHALL was vice president during both of Wilson's terms, 1913-1921. He was born on March 14, 1854 in North Manchester, Wabash County, Indiana where he attended Wabash College. Marshall "read for the law," and began his practice in Columbia City, Indiana where he was known for his hard drinking.

He was also a leader in his church and well respected. When he later married Lois Kimsey, she helped him stop drinking. He was elected governor and went to the 1912 Democratic nominating convention as Indiana's "favorite son" candidate. Marshall thought he had a chance as a compromise candidate, but when the convention went to the 46th ballot, he threw his votes to Wilson in return for the vice presidential spot.

Wilson did not take him into his confidence or involve him in the momentous events of the war or the creation of the League of Nations. When Wilson suffered a devastating stroke, a power vacuum was created which was filled by Wilson's wife.

Marshall returned to Indiana after his second term, saying, "I don't want to work (but) I wouldn't mind being vice president again." He died while visiting Washington on June 1, 1925 and is buried in Crown Hill Cemetery, Indianapolis, Indiana.

Appendix 2

The Wives of the Presidents

Martha Washington

Martha (Dandridge) Custis married George Washington on January 6, 1759. She was the widow of Daniel Parke Custis and had four children from that first marriage. Only two were surviving at the time of her marriage to Washington, who raised them as his own.

She never attended a formal school and at the time of her marriage to Washington had not traveled outside Virginia. She inherited from Custis a Williamsburg house, 1500 acres and 200 slaves, which combined with Washington's estate made him one of the richest men in Virginia.

She was born on June 2, 1731, in New Kent County, Virginia, at the White House, her family's plantation home. She died on May 22, 1802, at Mount Vernon where she is buried. Martha Washington was enthusiastic and friendly, and preferred a private life, but bravely followed the political path chosen by her husband, even to the severe winter encampments during the Revolution.

She wrote to a friend that she was "determined to be cheerful and happy...that the greater part of our happiness or misery depends upon our dispositions and not upon our circumstances."

Martha Jefferson

Martha (Wayles) Skelton married Thomas Jefferson on January 1, 1772. She was the widow of Bathurst Skelton and had a small son who died shortly before the marriage to Jefferson. She had six children with Jefferson, but only two daughters lived to adulthood.

She was born between October 19-30, 1748 in Charles City County, Virginia. Called "Patty" by her family, she died from complications of childbirth after a four month illness on September 6, 1782, and is buried at Monticello.

On her death bed, she and Jefferson copied together the lines from *Tristam Shandy*. She wrote, "Time wastes too fast: every letter I trace tells me with what rapidity life follows my pen; the days and hours of it...are flying over our heads like light clouds of a windy day never to return..." Jefferson finished, "...and every time I kiss thy hand to bid adieu, every absence which follows it, are preludes to that eternal separation which we are shortly to make."

Details of their life together is scant. Jefferson burned all the letters and papers between them, but 44 years later, after Jefferson's death, his daughter Martha (Patsy) found the death bed poem hidden in a private cabinet, its creases worn from frequent handling.

Dolley Madison

Dolley (Payne) Todd married James Madison on September 15, 1794. She had two children from her marriage to John Todd, Jr. He had died of yellow fever along with their youngest child. She and Madison were childless, but he raised her surviving son as his own.

She was born May 20, 1768, in (now) Guilford County, North Carolina, and died on July 12, 1849, in Washington, D.C. She is buried at Montpelier in the Madison family graveyard.

Her vivacious personality made her one of the most popular of all first ladies. Since Thomas Jefferson was a widower, she served on occasions as his hostess at White House functions while James Madison was Secretary of State.

When the British attacked and burned the White House in 1814, she escaped with the silver, red curtains, official papers and the famous Gilbert Stuart painting of George Washington, which hangs today in the White House.

After Madison's death, she returned to Washington and in 1844, the House of Representatives assigned her a permanent seat in Congressional Hall, the only first lady so honored.

She is buried in the Madison Family Cemetery at Montpelier.

Elizabeth Monroe

Elizabeth Kortright married James Monroe on February 16, 1786. They had three children, two daughters and an infant son who died. She was born on June 30, 1768 in New York City and died on September 23, 1830, at Oak Hill, Loudoun County, Virginia. In 1903, her remains were removed from Oak Hill and laid beside those of her husband in Hollywood Cemetery, Richmond, Virginia.

During the French Revolution, when her husband was minister to France, Elizabeth Monroe bravely visited the imprisoned wife of the Marquis de Lafayette and it is believed this interest was the reason the Marquise was spared from the guillotine. Elizabeth Monroe was known in France as *la belle Americaine.*

It is the family tradition that after her death Monroe burned all the correspondence of their life together.

Anna Harrison

Anna Tuthill Symmes secretly married William Henry Harrison, a young army officer on November 25, 1795, because her father resisted a marriage that would take her to a life of frontier forts. They would have ten children.

She was born on July 25, 1775, at Flatbrook, Sussex County, New Jersey and died on February 25, 1864, at North Bend, Ohio. She is buried in William Henry Harrison Memorial Park, North Bend, Ohio.

Anna Harrison was an invalid when her husband was elected president. She did not go to Washington, but gave the responsibility of White House hostess to her son's widow, Jane Findlay Irwin Harrison.

Letitia Tyler

Letitia Christian married John Tyler on March 29, 1813 at Cedar Grove in New Kent County, Virginia. They had three sons and five daughters. She was born on November 12, 1790, in New Kent County, Virginia, and died September 10, 1842, in Washington, D.C. and is buried in Cedar Grove Cemetery, New Kent County, Virginia.

Known for a gentle and gracious manner, she was an invalid at the time of her husband's election in 1841, and was the first wife of a president to die in the White House.

Her duties were assumed by Priscilla, wife of her eldest son Robert. Later, the mistress of the White House was the second daughter, Letitia. Both were aided by the advice of Dolley Madison, living nearby in Washington.

Julia Tyler

Julia Gardiner married John Tyler on June 26, 1844, in New York. They had seven children. She was born on July 23, 1820, on Gardiner's Island, New York and died on July 10, 1889, in Richmond, where she is buried beside her husband in Hollywood Cemetery. She was thirty years Tyler's junior and her marriage to the president interested the nation. She deftly handled her roles as hostess at the White House, and at the end of his presidency, as mistress of the plantation, Sherwood Forest.

John Tyler died as civil war ripped apart the Union, which left her impoverished, but she remained devoted to her adopted state.

Margaret Taylor

Margaret Mackall Smith married Zachary Taylor on June 21, 1810. They had one son and five daughters, but two of the girls died in infancy. She was born on September 21, 1788, in Calvert County, Maryland, and died on August 14, 1852, in East Pascagoula, Mississippi and is buried in Zachary Taylor National Cemetery, Louisville, Kentucky.

As the wife of an army officer, much of her life was spent at remote army posts on the frontier. At the time of her husband's election as president, she was in failing health.

She enjoyed small gatherings, but as first lady, she shunned social occasions, designating as official White House hostess her youngest daughter, Mary Elizabeth, also the wife of an army officer.

She was a devout Episcopalian and while in Washington DC daily attended St. John's Episcopal Church across Lafayette Square.

Ellen Wilson

Ellen Louise Axson married Woodrow Wilson on June 24, 1885 and they had three daughters. She was born on May 15, 1860, in Savannah, Georgia and died on August 6, 1914, in the White House from Bright's Disease and is buried at Myrtle Hill Cemetery in Rome, Georgia.

She was devoted to her husband's academic career and later to his decisions to run for governor of New Jersey and president. One of her first acts at the White House was to plant a rose garden near the Oval Office.

She was already an accomplished portrait painter when she married. This was put aside, but when her daughters became older she began painting landscapes. She donated the proceeds from sales of her paintings to fund scholarships at the Berry School for the education of rural mountain children.

She used her influence as first lady to improve the living conditions of the poor in Washington, D.C. and the working conditions of women.

Edith Wilson

Edith (Bolling) Galt married Woodrow Wilson on December 18, 1915. They had no children. She was born in Wytheville, Virginia, on October 15, 1872, and died on December 28, 1961, and is buried with her husband in Washington Cathedral, Washington, D.C.

When Wilson became paralyzed by a stroke, in the middle of his second term, she shielded him from all public contact for a period of more than six months. She was labeled the "secret president," and exercised enormous power. Her role was highly controversial although she termed her involvement as a "stewardship."

Appendix 3

Planning the Trip

Sites previously described in the narrative as not open to the public are not included.

WASHINGTON, D.C.

Washington, District of Columbia

The northern states wanted the capital city to remain in a northern city while the southern states wanted it located near the center of the new country. Congress worked out a compromise which designated a section along the Potomac north of Georgetown. Washington wanted it closer to the town of Alexandria and Congress agreed. The capital of the new nation was formed by a ten mile square from parts of Maryland and Virginia and it was called the District of Columbia. Washington laid the cornerstone of the new Capitol building in 1793. The capital city in the District of Columbia was named in honor of George Washington and the boundaries of the city and the District are identical. The Virginia portion was eventually returned and became Arlington County. The French engineer, Major Pierre Charles L'Enfant designed the city before any buildings were erected. One of the conditions for locating the capital on the Potomac was that it remain in New York for eighteen months and then in Philadelphia until 1800. In that year, Congress and the government offices moved to the new city of Washington. John Adams occupied the White House for the last year of his term and Thomas Jefferson was the first president inaugurated in the new capital city. There, the **Washington Monument** soars far above the other buildings. A short distance away, across the tidal basin, sits the dome of the **Jefferson Memorial** and nearby is the **George Mason Memorial.** Down the mall is the memorial to the **Signers of the Declaration of Independence.** Behind the Capitol Building is the **Library of Congress** and in the middle of the city is **The President**

Woodrow Wilson House, the house on S street. Not far from the White House is the *Octagon House.*

Visitors: Traffic congestion and inadequate parking in Washington make visiting the sites by car difficult. The Metro system, www.dcvisit.com, or a tour bus is recommended.

Directions: Washington is located on the Potomac River and can be reached from I-95 or I-66 or many of the exits on I-495 which circles the city. Metro stop: Federal Triangle on the Blue line.

Contact: D. C. Visitor Information Center, 1300 Pennsylvania Avenue, N.W., The Ronald Reagan International Trade Center Building, Ground Floor, Washington, D.C. 20004; (202) 328-4748, (800) 422-8644; washington.org

NORTHERN VIRGINIA

Alexandria

On land purchased in 1669 by John Alexander, for "six thousand pounds of Tobacco and Cask," the City of Alexandria, then called Belle Haven, became an important port on the Potomac River. In 1749, the House of Burgesses incorporated the town and named it in honor of the Alexander family. A young George Washington, then living in his brother's home at Mount Vernon, assisted the surveyor who laid out the streets. The old town section of the city has been restored and its shops and restaurants are popular with tourists. Located within the city are the *National Masonic Memorial, Christ Church, the Presbyterian Meeting House,* and *Gadsby's Tavern.*

Visitors: Contact the Ramsay House Visitors Center for brochures, map, reservations and guidance. Old Town Alexandria is a central place to start when visiting the various Alexandria and Fairfax sites as well as the monuments in Washington, D.C.

Directions: Alexandria is on the Potomac River, a few

miles south of Washington, D.C. on Virginia Route 1. It can be reached from I-95 or I-395.

Contact: Ramsay House Visitors Center, 221 King St., Alexandria, Virginia 22314-3209; (703) 746-3301 or (800) 388-9119

Fairfax County

All the land between the Potomac and Rappahannock Rivers was granted by King Charles II in 1649. Called the Northern Neck Grant, it came under the control of Thomas, Sixth Lord of Fairfax. He came to Virginia and built his home Greenway Court in Frederick County. In 1732, the General Assembly created Truro Parish from northern Prince William County. Lord Fairfax took this as his personal estate and ten years later the boundaries of the parish were used to designate Fairfax County. On its eastern tip with its dazzling view of the Potomac sits *Mount Vernon* and on its western boundary is the *Patowmack Canal* in Great Falls Park. Between Mount Vernon and Alexandria is *River Farm*. South of Mount Vernon is *Washington's Grist Mill, Woodlawn and Pohick Church.* Farther south on the Potomac is *Gunston Hall.*

Visitors: These sites must be visited by car. Except for the Patowmack Canal, the sites in Fairfax County are located along U. S. Route 1. The Fairfax County Visitors Center is open daily (except Thanksgiving and Christmas) from 10:00 a.m. to 6:00 p.m. and Sunday 11:00 a.m. to 6:00 p.m. Download Visitors Guide at http://guides.milespartnership.com/fax/14/index.html

Contact: Fairfax County/Capital Region Visitors Center, 1961 Chain Bridge Road, McLean, VA 22102 (Tysons Corner Shopping Center); (703) 752-9500 or 800-732-4732; www.fxva.com/seedoplan/visitor-centers/

Fredericksburg

Located near the falls of the Rappahannock River, Fredericksburg became an inland port in 1728. George Washington spent his youth at *Ferry Farm* just east of Fredericksburg on Route 3. After his mother became too old to stay on the farm, he purchased a home for her in Fredericksburg, now called the *Mary Washington House.* Her burial site and monument is nearby. *Historic Kenmore*, the home of George Washington's sister Betty Washington Lewis, contains some of the finest woodwork and design of any antebellum home. James Monroe practiced law in Fredericksburg and the *James Monroe Museum* is located on the site where his office once stood. There is also the *Thomas Jefferson Religious Freedom Monument* at the intersection of Washington Avenue and Pitt Street.

Visitors: The best way to see Fredericksburg is to stop at the Visitors Center on Caroline Street, where there is free parking and a 15 minute movie presentation. Open daily from 9:00 a.m. to 5:00 p.m. and Sunday from 11:00 a.m. to 5:00 p.m. A narrated trolley tour (one hour and fifteen minutes) departs from the Visitors Center. The city sites are within walking distance.

Directions: Fredericksburg can be reached from I-95 or Virginia State Route 1. Take Virginia Route 3 which runs through the center of town and becomes William Street. There are signs to guide you to the Old Town and Visitors Center.

Contact: Fredericksburg Visitor's Center, 706 Caroline Street, Fredericksburg, Virginia 22401; (540) 373-1776 or (800) 678-4748; See also http://www.visitfred.com/

Westmoreland County

Refugees from the English civil war in the mid-seventeenth century swelled the population in Virginia's "Northern Neck," that area between the Potomac and Rappahannock Rivers. Pushing gradually westward beyond the reach of court and government, the settlers created a need for a new county seat. Named for a place in England, Westmoreland was formed in 1653 out of the western end of Northumberland County. Two Virginia presidents were born here. George Washington is commemorated by his reconstructed birth home at **Popes Creek**. James Monroe's birth home has disappeared but there is an obelisk marking the site of **Monroe Hall**.

Visitors: Both sites are accessible by car. Popes Creek has a visitors center, walking paths and picnic areas.

Directions: Go east from Fredericksburg on Virginia Route 3 to Oak Grove, then north on Virginia Route 205 for about 4 miles to Monroe Hall marker on right. Return to Route 3 and proceed east to Popes Creek. See map at http://visitwestmorelandva.com/maps.html#/Map

Contact: Westmoreland County Administration, P. O. Box 1000, Montross, Virginia 22520; (804) 493-0130; www.westmoreland-county.org/index.php?p=home

THE PIEDMONT

Richmond

Several days after landing at Jamestown, Christopher Newport sailed up the James River about sixty miles to the falls. A small cross was erected on one of the islands at the falls and later a fort was built. Richmond lies on the "fall line" which separates Virginia's Piedmont from the Tidewater. The fall line is roughly along the I-95 route A cross has been recreated at the end of 12th Street on the Canal Walk. This was the territory of the Powhatan tribe and in 1622 they wiped out all English settlements except Jamestown. The need for new land for tobacco drove the colonists west shoving the Indians across the Blue Ridge Mountains. In 1730, the Warehouse Act designated the development at the Falls of the James as an inspection station. Tobacco was brought to the station and loaded onto ships for export. It was not until 1737 that the area was surveyed by William Mayo. Called Richmond, after Richmond, England, King George I granted William Byrd a charter to establish the city in 1742. Richmond became the Virginia capital in 1780 while Thomas Jefferson was governor. **St. John's Episcopal Church**, built in 1741, was the place where Patrick Henry defied the British with his "Give me liberty or give me death" speech. The **State Capitol** was constructed under the direction of Thomas Jefferson and the General Assembly first met their in 1792 In its rotunda is the magnificent **Houdon statue of Washington** surrounded by busts of the seven other Virginia Presidents. West of the city is **Tuckahoe Plantation.** Exhibits of interest may be found at the Virginia Historical Society, 428 North Boulevard; www.vahistorical.org/, and at the Library of Virginia, 800 E. Broad Street; www.lva.lib.va.us. At **Hollywood Cemetery** are the graves of **James Monroe** and **John Tyler.**

Visitors: Parking and street directions are visitor friendly; Official Visitor Center, open daily from 9:00 a.m. to 5:00 p.m.

Directions: Richmond is in the center of Virginia at the intersection of I-95 and I-64.

Contact: Official Visitor Center of Richmond, 405 North 3rd Street, Richmond, Virginia 23219; (804) 783-7450. www.visitrichmondva.com/plan-your-trip/visitor-center/

Charlottesville

Notched Road or Three Chopped Road - named for the cuts on the trees to mark the way - was started in 1733 to run from Richmond to the Blue Ridge. It was surveyed by Peter Jefferson, father of Thomas Jefferson. In 1762, the General Assembly authorized a town to be named after Charlotte of Mecklenburg-Strelitz, Queen of England and wife to George III, to be laid out in a 56 acre tract on the Notched Road. The road today is in the general location of Virginia Route 250 which in Charlottesville becomes Main Street. Located in Charlottesville is Jefferson's **"academical village,"** the University of Virginia. James Monroe's "lower plantation" in the area of **Monroe Hill** was absorbed into the campus where his law office was located. East of Charlottesville is **Monticello,** Thomas Jefferson's birthplace and home. Nearby is **Ash Lawn-Highland,** the home of James Monroe.

Visitors: Go first to the Charlottesville/Albemarle Convention and Visitor's Bureau at 610 East Main Street, Charlottesville. It is open from 9:00 a.m. to 5:00 p.m. daily. Inquire about the discount pass for Monticello, Ash Lawn-Highland, and Michie Tavern and reservations services for local hotels.

Directions: Charlottesville is east of the Blue Ridge and can be reached from I-64 or Virginia Routes 29 and 250.

Contact: Charlottesville/Albemarle Convention and Visitor's Bureau, P. O. Box 178, Charlottesville, Virginia 22902; (434) 293-6789 or (877) 386-1103; www.visitcharlottesville.org/about/cvb/

Orange County

Orange County was created in 1732 by taking that portion of Spotsylvania County north of Hanover County and south of the grant to Lord Fairfax. Its western boundary was the Mississippi River. The new county was named for William of Orange, the future William III. In Orange County are the roots of the Madison and Taylor families and their homes, *Montpelier*, James Madison's home, and *Barboursville ruins*, designed by Thomas Jefferson. In the town of Orange is the *James Madison Museum.*

Visitors: First visit the James Madison Museum and then drive about 10 minutes to Montpelier.

Directions: Orange is at the junction of Virginia Route 20 and U. S. Route 15. It can be reached from U. S. Route 29 by Virginia Route 33, then north on Virginia Route 20, or Route 20 north from Charlottesville. From I-95, west on Virginia Route 3 to Virginia Route 20.

Contact: Orange County Department of Tourism and Visitor's Bureau, 122 E. Main Street, Orange, VA 22960; (540) 672-1653 or (877) 222-8072; www.visitorangevirginia.com/

Bedford County

Bedford County was formed in 1754. In 1782, the town of Liberty was founded, but 98 years later, it became the

City of Bedford. It was in this county that Thomas Jefferson built *Poplar Forest* on a tract of land inherited by his wife.

Directions: Bedford County is south west of Lynchburg. It is about a two hour drive south on U. S. Route 29 from Charlottesville, then west on U. S. Route 460.

Contact: Bedford Tourism and Welcome Center, 816 Burks Hill Road, Bedford, Virginia 24523; (540) 587-5681 or (877) 447-3257; www.visitbedford.com

THE SHENANDOAH VALLEY

Lexington

In 1778, a small place known as Gilbert Campbell's Ford was renamed Lexington in honor of the first battle of the Revolutionary War. Lexington is in the upper Shenandoah Valley. It is located in Rockbridge County which takes its name from the *Natural Bridge,* located on a tract of land owned by Thomas Jefferson. Here, George Washington endowed the small school that became *Washington and Lee University.*

Directions: Lexington is easily reached by I-64 and I-81.

Contact: Lexington-Rockbridge County Chamber of Commerce, 106 East Washington Street, Lexington, Virginia 24450; (540) 463-3777; www.lexingtonvirginia.com

Staunton

Staunton is in the Shenandoah Valley, the gateway west through the Blue Ridge to the Allegheny Mountains. Settled in 1732 it was named for Lady Rebecca Staunton, wife of Governor William Gooch. Staunton did not suffer great destruction during the Civil War, so much of its early architecture is intact. Here is the *Birthplace of Woodrow Wilson.*

Directions: Staunton is located at the junction of I-64 and I-81 about one hour west over the Blue Ridge from Charlottesville.

Contact: Staunton Convention and Visitors Bureau, 116 West Beverly Street, Staunton, Virginia 24401; (540) 332-3865 (or 800-342-3972); www.staunton.va.us

Winchester

Winchester was first known as Frederick Town. It was originally settled by Germans and Scottish-Irish from Pennsylvania and was officially founded as the first city west of the Blue Ridge in 1744 by Colonel James Wood. Wood changed the name to Winchester, the place of his birth in England. Here is *Washington's Headquarters* and nearby is *Belle Grove Plantation.*

Visitors: The sites in Winchester related to George Washington can be walked or driven. Maps and memorabilia are available at the Visitor Center.

Directions: Winchester lies in the lower Shenandoah Valley and can be reached from I-81 or I-66.

Contact: Winchester-Frederick County Visitor Center, 1400 S. Pleasant Valley Road, Winchester, Virginia 22601; (540) 542-1326 or (877) 871-1326; www.visitwinchesterva.org

THE TIDEWATER

Williamsburg

Middle Plantation was an outpost to guard against Indian attacks on the capital at Jamestown. Located on the peninsula between the James and the York Rivers, it became the Virginia capital in 1699 and was named Williamsburg for King William III of England. The *College of William and Mary* had been established in 1695 and the main street of the new city, the Duke of Marlborough Street, started at the front of the main college building, named for Christopher Wren, and went to the Capitol building. Williamsburg remained Virginia's capital for eighty years, but in 1780 it was moved to Richmond. Williamsburg remained a functioning city, although many of the original buildings had been replaced or were in a state of disrepair when John D. Rockefeller, Jr. agreed in 1926 to finance its restoration. Today, the Historic Area of Williamsburg is operated by the Colonial Williamsburg Foundation. Located within the city are the **College of William and Mary which educated three of the Virginia presidents, the Magazine, where the Royal Governor** tried to seize the colonists' gunpowder, the *Capitol*, where Patrick Henry made his "If this be treason..." speech and the *Raleigh Tavern* where the delegates assembled in the First Virginia Convention after the Governor dissolved the House of Burgesses.

Visitors: Colonial Williamsburg may be visited every day of the year but advance reservations are recommended. There are signs to the Colonial Williamsburg Information Center. East along the John Tyler Memorial Highway (Virginia Route 5) are *Berkeley* and *Sherwood Forest.*, and other "James River plantations."

Directions: One of the points on the "Golden Triangle," Williamsburg is at the halfway point of the Colonial Parkway which provides access to Jamestown and Yorktown. Williamsburg can be reached by Route 5, the John Tyler Memorial Highway, or by I-64 from Richmond or Norfolk, take exit 238, Route 143, then right on 132 to the Visitors Center.

Contact: Colonial Williamsburg Regional Visitor Center, 101 Visitor Center Dr.ive, Williamsburg, Virginia 23185; (888) 965– 7254; http://www.colonialwilliamsburg.com/plan/visitor-center/

Jamestown

The first settlers landed at *Cape Henry* at the mouth of the Chesapeake Bay and erected a cross and then moved to a site called Point Comfort (now, Old Point Comfort). They explored up the James for approximately two weeks and on May 14, 1607, selected an island in the river and constructed a fort, which they called James Fort, for King James I, The early Jamestown inhabitants came for gold and other riches and had little organization or civic discipline. John Smith provided strong leadership at first, but he returned to England. The challenge of the wilderness shrunk the 500 inhabitants to 60 in the winter of 1609-1610, referred to as "the starving time." New leadership from England and the discovery of a crop for export - tobacco - put the colony back on its feet, and it became *Jamestown* in 1619. In 1624, James I revoked the charter of the Virginia Company of London, and Virginia became a royal colony. Jamestown was the Virginia capital until 1699 when it was moved to Williamsburg. The original Jamestown settlement slowly disappeared, but in a remarkable archaeological endeavor, has been discovered and re-created. *Jamestown Settlement* is operated by the Commonwealth of Virginia. *Historic Jamestown—America's Birthplace* is part of Colonial National Historical Park and is managed by the National Park Service.

Visitors: Both sites should be visited. Access by car is visitor friendly.

Directions: One of the points on the "Golden Triangle," Jamestown is at the end of the Colonial Parkway which provides access to Williamsburg and Yorktown. From I-64 take exit 242A, then Route 199 west to the Colonial Parkway. It can also be reached by Virginia Route 5, then south on Virginia Route 31.

Contact: Colonial National Historical Park, P.O. Box 210, Yorktown, Virginia 23690; (757) 898-2410; www.nps.gov/ colo/index.htm; Jamestown-Yorktown Foundation, P.O. Box 1607, Williamsburg, Virginia 23187-1607 (757) 253-4838 or (888) 593-4682; www.historyisfun.org

Yorktown

One of the original eight Virginia shires (but always referred to as counties), York was first called Charles River. Originally named for Charles I, it was changed in 1642 for his son James, Duke of York. Bordered on the north by the York River, the county's port became the shipping point for the tobacco trade. Established in 1691 by the Virginia House of Burgesses, an Act of Ports designated **Yorktown** as port for trade and customs. When tobacco failed in the mid 1700's, Yorktown was largely abandoned. In 1881, when Cornwallis waited in vain for the British fleet, much of the town was destroyed by cannon fire. The battle of Yorktown is told at two sites, **Yorktown Victory Center** and **Yorktown National Battlefield.**

Visitors: Yorktown is one of the points of the "Golden Triangle" with Williamsburg and Jamestown. Access by car is visitor friendly. Visit the Yorktown Victory Center, then go to the National Park Visitor Center for a guided or self-guided tour of the town. There are self-guided automobile tours of the battlefield. Ask about combination tickets.

Directions: Yorktown is at one end of the Colonial Parkway. It can also be reached from I-64, eastbound is exit 242B and westbound is exit 247B.

Contact: See the articles on the Victory Center and Battlefield Visitor Center.

Virginia Beach

Where the Chesapeake meets the Atlantic Ocean are the Virginia Capes. Today, the two are connected by the Chesapeake Bay Bridge Tunnel. It was here that Admiral de Grasse blocked the British fleet from Yorktown. The **Cape Henry Memorial** is the memorial cross marking the site where the Jamestown colonists first landed on April 26, 1607.

Visitors: Entrance to the Cape Henry Memorial is through the Fort Story gate 8 (Joint Expeditionary Base Little Creek) at the north end of Virginia Beach on Atlantic Avenue.

Directions: From Richmond take I-64 to its junction with I-264 then east into Virginia Beach, then north on U. S. Route 60 to Fort Story. **Great Dismal Swamp** is approximately 25 miles west of Virginia Beach on I-264.

Contact: Colonial National Historical Park, P. O. Box 210, Yorktown, Virginia 23690; (757) 898-2410; www.nps.gov/came/planyourvisit/directions.htm

Appendix 4

Map of Virginia (partial)

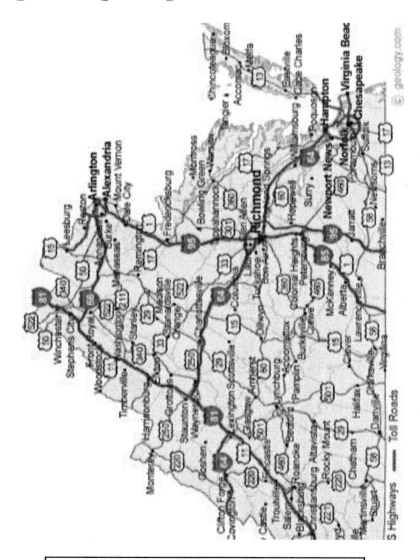

Calculate distance, time and directions:
http://distancecalculator.globefeed.com/
us_Distance_Calculator.asp?state=VA

Appendix 5

Bibliographical Essay

For those who may wish more information on the lives of the Virginia presidents, the following suggestions can be a starting point.

British America

The Spanish, French and English movements in North America are mapped in *The American Heritage Pictorial Atlas* (American Heritage, 1966). For the influence of the European Enlightenment on British America's political and social thought, a classic exposition is *The Empire of Reason,* by Henry Steel Commager (Phoenix Press, 2000). The founding of the Jamestown Colony is told in *Captain John Smith and the Jamestown Story,* by Lauran Paine (Hippocrene Books, 1973). An archaeologist's search for America's birthplace is in *The Virginia Adventure: Roanoke to Jamestown An Archaeological and Historical Odyssey,* by Ivor Noël Hume (Alfred A. Knopf, 1994).

Rebellion

A very readable narrative account of the events which led to the Revolution is *A Struggle for Power: The American Revolution,* by Theodore Draper (Times Books, 1966). How the mind of the colonist moved from loyalty to rebellion is best told in the classic Pulitzer prize winning *The Ideological Origins of the American Revolution,* by Bernard Bailyn (The Belnap Press of Harvard University Press, 1992).

George Washington

Of course, the books on Washington overwhelm even the dedicated reader. There are many one volume biographies but one of the most readable is *George Washington,* by John R. Alden (Wings Books, 1995). A different approach which illuminates Washington's character is *Founding Father,* by Richard Brookhiser (The Free Press, 1969). The presidential years are recounted in *The Presidency of George Washington,* by Forest McDonald (University Press of Kansas, 1974). Different aspects of Washington's character are in the anthology *George Washington Reconsidered,* edited by Don Higginbotham (The University Press of Virginia, 2001). *George Washington, A Biographical Companion.* by Frank E. Grizzard, Jr. (ABC-Clio, Inc., 2002) is a reference work on many aspects of Washington's life. For a narrative account of the revolution, *The Glorious Cause,* by Robert Middlekauff (Oxford University Press, 1982) is a terrific one volume treatment, which also explains briefly why war came. For a helpful book to carry if one wishes to visit the battle sites, there is *American Battlefields,* by Hubbard Cobb (MacMillan, 1995). Online for The Papers of George Washington, at http://founders.archives.gov/ See also, George Washington Papers at the Library of Congress, http://memory.loc.gov/ammem/gwhtml/

Thomas Jefferson

The material on Jefferson can be described as a deluge, but the seminal biography remains *Jefferson and His Time,* by Dumas Malone, in six volumes (Little, Brown & Company, 1948). For a reduced Jefferson in one volume, see *Thomas Jefferson and the New Nation,* by Merrill D. Peterson (Oxford University Press, 1970) or, *In Pursuit of Reason, The Life of Thomas Jefferson,* by Noble E. Cunningham, Jr. (Louisiana State University Press, 1987). Other one volume treatments include *Thomas Jefferson and Slavery,* by John Chester Miller (The Free Press, 1977) and *Thomas Jefferson: A Life,* by Willard Sterne Randall (Henry Holt and Company, 1973), which relates the charming story of the poem recited by Martha and Thomas Jefferson in her last days. The issues faced by Jefferson in his two terms are discussed in *The Presidency of Thomas Jefferson,* by Forest McDonald (University Press of Kansas, 1976). An excellent survey of the events and persons in Jefferson's era is *Thomas Jefferson, A Biographical Companion,* by David S. Brown (ABC-Clio

192

1998). Jefferson's role in classical courthouse design is in *Virginia's Historic Courthouses,* John O. and Margaret Peters (University Press of Virginia, 1996). For the story of what happened to Monticello after Jefferson's death, see *Saving Monticello: The Levy Family's Epic Quest to Rescue the House that Jefferson Built,* by Marc Leepson (Free Press 2001). For the story of Poplar Forest, see *Poplar Forest and Thomas Jefferson,* S. Allen Chambers, Jr. (The Corporation for Jefferson's Poplar Forest, 1998). No issue has so roiled the Jefferson legacy as Monticello's position on Sally Hemings. The most thorough and evenhanded examination is *The Jefferson-Hemings Controversy: Report of the Scholars Commission,* edited by Robert F. Turner (Carolina Academic Press 2001, 2011).

James Madison

Although called the "Father of the Constitution," James Madison seems under recognized as the architect of the American system of government. His standard biography is *James Madison: A Biography,* by Ralph Ketcham (University Press of Virginia, 1990). His presidential years as well as his conflict with Virginia's "old republicans" is told in *The Presidency of James Madison,* by Robert Allen Rutland, (University Press of Kansas, 1990). There are many accounts on the writing of the Constitution, but perhaps the most readable narrative remains the classic *Miracle at Philadelphia: the Story of the Constitutional Convention, May to September 1787,* by Catherine Drinker Bowen (Atlantic-Little, Brown Books, 1966). *Novus Ordo Seclorum, The Intellectual Origins of the Constitution,* by Forest McDonald (University Press of Kansas, 1985) is a compelling analysis of the historical thought which the Founding Fathers brought to the making of the Constitution. An overview of the issue not named in the Constitution - slavery - is *American Slavery ... American Freedom,* by Edmund S. Morgan (W. W. Norton & Co., 1975).

James Monroe

James Monroe's long and important public career is told in *James Monroe: The Quest for National Identity*, by Henry Ammon (University Press of Virginia, 1990). *The Political Writings of James Monroe*, by James P. Lucier, has informative biographical introductions on the phases of Monroe's career. A recounting of Monroe's two terms is *The Presidency of James Monroe*, by Noble E. Cunningham, Jr. (The University Press of Kansas, 1996).

William Henry Harrison

The long army career of William Henry Harrison is also the story of the displacement of the Indians in the first half of the 19th century and the early Indian wars, told in *Old Tippecanoe: William Henry Harrison and His Time,* by Freeman Cleaves (American Political Biography Press, 1967). The history and conquest of the native inhabitants of the American continent is wonderfully researched in *The Indian Heritage of America,* by Alvin M. Josephy, Jr. (Alfred A. Knopf, 1970).

John Tyler

The best account of John Tyler's presidency and the self assuredness of his personality is in *The Presidencies of William Henry Harrison and John Tyler,* by Norma Lois Peterson (University Press of Kansas, 1989). A somewhat out of date style still conveys the importance of John Tyler's role in the evolution of the presidency is *John Tyler: Champion of the Old South*, by Oliver Perry Chitwood (American Political Biography Press, 1990). Other details can be found in *And Tyler Too: A Biography of John and* Julia *Gardiner Tyler*, by Robert Seager II (McGraw-Hill, 1963). A look at the forces that shaped Tyler's presidency is *The Republican Vision of John Tyler*, by Dan Monroe (Texas A & M University Press 2003).

Zachary Taylor

Zachary Taylor's life is also the story of Manifest Destiny, America's western march to the Pacific, told in *Zachary Taylor: Soldier, Planter, Statesman of the Old Southwest*, by K. Jack Bauer (Louisiana State University Press, 1985).

Woodrow Wilson

With Woodrow Wilson, the presidency finds a challenge to the constitutional structure of government. His life is ably covered in the Pulitzer Prize winning *Woodrow Wilson*, by Arthur Walworth (W. W. Norton & Company, Inc., 1958). An excellent one volume history of Wilson as president is *The Presidency of Woodrow Wilson*, by Kendrick A. Clements (University Press of Kansas, 1992). For those who wish the details of the American effort in World War I, there is the highly readable *The Doughboys: The Story of the AEF, 1917-1918*, by Laurence Stallings (Harper & Row, Publishers, 1963). What happened at Versailles is detailed in *End of Order: Versailles 1919*, by Charles L. Mee, Jr. (E. P. Dalton, 1980). Wilson's illness as a cause of the League's rejection by the U. S. Congress, from the perspective of Wilson's second marriage, is in *Edith and Woodrow: The Wilson White House*, by Phyllis Lee Levin (Scribner, 2001).

Appendix 6

Images

Montpelier

>Picture provided courtesy of The Montpelier Foundation

Grouseland

>Picture provided courtesy Grouseland Foundation

Berkeley

>Picture provided courtesy Berkeley Plantation

The President Woodrow Wilson House

>Picture provided courtesy of the President Woodrow Wilson House – a site of the National Trust for Historic Preservation

Pictures taken by the author:

Mount Vernon

>Courtesy of Mount Vernon Estate and Gardens

George Washington Masonic National Memorial

>Courtesy of George Washington Masonic National Memorial Association

Houdon Statue of Washington

>Courtesy of the General Assembly of Virginia

Monticello

>Courtesy of Thomas Jefferson Foundation

Barboursville Ruins

>Courtesy Barboursville Vineyards and Historic Ruins

Cresson Bust of Monroe

>Courtesy of James Monroe Museum and Memorial Library

Sherwood Forest

>Courtesy of Sherwood Forest Plantation

Wilson Birthplace Home

>Courtesy of Wilson Birthplace Foundation

Index

About the author:

Richard E Dixon is a graduate of Duke University and the University of Virginia Law School. He practiced law in Fairfax County and is now retired to Clifton, Virginia. He is the President of the Thomas Jefferson Heritage Society.

TheViriginiaPresidents.com